Dedication:

To all of the colleagues who, over a p[...] with me their love of teaching and their [...] and Todd with whom I worked in the Int[...] at Vanguard High School in recognition of their exemplary professionalism and their friendship.

Acknowledgements:

I am indebted to numerous editors and critics as I have acknowledged in the Bibliography. Where I am conscious of having taken an idea from a particular place, I have cited the source in the text.

Thanks to John for reading the manuscript and making invaluable suggestions, and (as always) to Barbara for preparing the manuscript for publication. The errors that remain are my own.

Readers who are familiar with my book *"The General Prologue" by Geoffrey Chaucer: A Critical Introduction* will notice that I have adapted some material from that work (particularly in the Preface, Introduction, the first two chapters, and Appendix Two). Except for the map on page 3, which is used by kind permission of the copyright holder, *all* images reproduced in this book are (to the best of my knowledge) in the public domain and therefore not subject to copyright. I believe that all quotations in the book fall under the definition of 'fair use.' If I am in error, please contact me by email: moore.ray1@yahoo.com

Main Illustrations:

Page 3: The map "London in 1381" is used by permission of John Simkin.
Page 7: The Pilgrims at the Tabard Inn reprinted from William Caxton's second edition of *The Canterbury Tales* (1483). Source: Wikipedia.
Page 11: Geoffrey Chaucer reprinted from *Historic Byways and Highways of Old England* (1900) by William Andrews. Source: AbeBooks.com.
Pilgrim images of the Wife of Bath (page 13) and the Friar (163), adapted from the Ellesmere Manuscript, reprinted from Alfred W. Pollard, *Chaucer's Canterbury Tales: The Prologue*, London: Macmillan (1903). Source: Free EBook, Google Books.
Page 149: *John Gower Takes Aim at the World*, a portrait from a book with his *Vox Clamantis* and *Chronica Tripertita.* Source: Manuscript in Glasgow Univ. Lib. Source: Wikipedia.
Page 154: Sir Gawain, Howard Pyle illustration from the 1903 edition of *The Story of King Arthur and His Knights*. Source: Wikimedia Commons.

Note: Illustrations which accompany the text are sourced and credited on the pages on which they appear.

The Wife of Bath's Prologue and Tale

by Geoffrey Chaucer

Text & Critical Introduction

by

Ray Moore M.A.

First Edition January 2014
Revised Edition April 2014
Copyright Ray Moore, 2014. All rights reserved.
ISBN Number: 978-1494850456

Contents

Preface

The ideal Chaucerian interpreter must combine the skills of medieval grammarian, literary historian, socio-political historian, and literary critic. I do not claim to qualify fully in any of these categories, but I do have fifty years' experience of reading, studying, and teaching Chaucer. Reading Middle English can be intimidating. The aim of this book is to take away the fear and leave you free to enjoy a remarkable piece of writing. It is a myth that only scholars can understand and appreciate a text written in Middle English.

This book is for the student who reads the *The Wife of Bath's Prologue and Tale* because it is on his/her syllabus, or for the general reader who simply wants to experience Chaucer. The analysis goes beyond that of the ubiquitous 'Notes' (helpful as they are to the first-time reader) whilst avoiding the esoteric language of the specialist academic literature.

Editions of the Middle English text are all pretty much the same with only minor variations in wording, spelling and line numbering. In editing the text, I have sought to make the meaning as clear as possible. The side-by-side modernization of the text does not keep to Chaucer's rhyme scheme or meter because doing so forces compromises on meaning. I have endeavored, as far as possible, to keep to the discipline of a line-by-line approach because this makes it easier to refer back to the Middle English text. For each line, I give the *full meaning* rather than a word-for-word 'translation,' and so I have frequently added details normally found in textual notes which I have reduced to a minimum.

The analysis of the text itself presents a coherent reading supported by references to relevant critical opinions. Where the interpretation offered is controversial, I present the arguments on each side and give my own interpretation. Readers will take what they find convincing and reject what they do not.

Middle English can seem daunting at first, but it is easier than it looks. There are many excellent commercial recordings of the *Wife of Bath's Prologue and Tale*. Get hold of one and listen to it while following along in the text; then read along with it; and finally read the text aloud by yourself. You will soon get the hang of it and find yourself able to read other Middle English texts.

Note: In revising the book I have been able to correct a few minor errors and to include more illustrations, none of which is, to the best of my knowledge, subject to copyright. If I am in error, please contact me by email: moore.ray1@yahoo.com

Chapter 1: A Game of Fiction

Southwark is today a London borough south of the River Thames. In Chaucer's time, there was only one bridge across the Thames, London Bridge, and it led from the still-walled city into Southwark. Not being under the control of the City of London authorities, Southwark had a reputation as being a rather lawless place where prostitution flourished. The totally respectable Tabard Inn was situated on the east side of the only road leading south, making it a popular gathering point for those planning to travel to Canterbury.

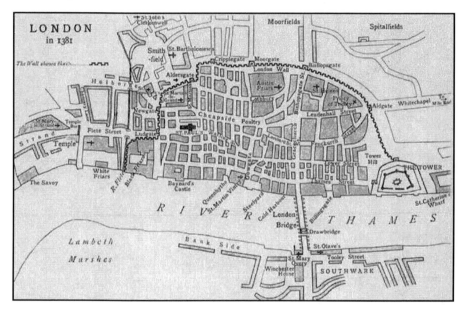

The frame story upon which Chaucer will build is presented in the early lines of the *General Prologue*:

> It happened that in spring one day,
> As I was staying at the Tabard Inn in Southwark
> Prior to setting out on my pilgrimage
> To Canterbury with a very devout heart,
> There came at night into that lodging
> Around twenty-nine folks in a company
> Of various classes of people who had fallen quite by chance
> Into fellowship, and they were all pilgrims
> Who intended to ride to Canterbury.
> The bedrooms and the stables were spacious,
> And we were excellently accommodated.

To be brief, by the time the sun had gone down,
I had spoken with every one of them to such effect that
I was accepted into their group straightway,
And had agreed to rise early,
To begin our journey, as I shall tell you.
(19-34 Author's modernization)

There is an interesting discrepancy between the number of pilgrims reported by the narrator and the number actually described in the *Prologue*. The number twenty-nine cannot possibly be right: counting the pilgrims mentioned in the text there are either twenty-eight or thirty. It all depends on the meaning of lines 163-4 which describe the retinue of the Prioress, "Another NONNE with hire hadde she, / That was hir chapeleyne, and preestes thre." Is the Prioress accompanied by one priest or by three? To me, three would make no sense at all. The lines indicate that the Prioress, the Second Nun and the Priest make a total of three. Thus, the Pilgrim joins a pre-existing group of twenty-eight. Why, then does the Pilgrim describe that group as being, "Wel nine and twenty in a compaigne" (24)? The first answer is that the word "Wel" indicates that the number is an approximation, 'twenty-nine or so.' Secondly, the number twenty-nine is probably used because it was on 29th December 1170 that Thomas Becket was murdered. Chaucer is thus the twenty-ninth pilgrim – a propitious number.

That same evening, over supper, the Host of The Tabard Inn, one Harry Bailey, proposes an entertainment which he guarantees will add to the pilgrims' pleasure on their journey to and from Canterbury:

"You go to Canterbury; may God speed you,
And may the blessed martyr reward you as you deserve!
I know well that as you go on your way,
You plan to tell tales and amuse yourselves,
For truly, there is neither comfort nor enjoyment
In riding along the way as dumb as a stone;
And therefore will I provide you with an amusement,
As I said before, to give you some pleasure.
And if you all agree unanimously
To be ruled by my judgment,
And to do exactly as I direct you,
Tomorrow, when you ride upon your way,
Then, by my father's soul, who is dead,
If you do not enjoy yourselves, I will give you my head!
Hold up your hands, without any more talk."
Our decision was not difficult to reach.
We thought it was not worth thinking too seriously about,

And we granted him his way without further discussion,
And bade him tell his plan if it pleased him.
"Masters," he stated, "listen carefully to something for your own advantage;
But do not, I beg of you, receive it scornfully.
This is the point, to put it briefly and plainly,
That each of you, to make our journey seem shorter,
Shall tell two stories as you wend your way
Towards Canterbury, that is my point,
And on the return journey each shall tell another two,
All of adventures which have happened in olden times.
And he who does this the best of all,
That is to say, who tells in this competition
The most morally meaningful and most entertaining tales,
Shall have a supper paid for by the others
Here in this place, sitting by this very post,
When we come back again from Canterbury.
And in order to add to your enjoyment,
I will myself gladly ride along with you,
Completely at my own cost and be your master of ceremonies;
But whosoever shall go against my rules
Shall pay for all that we spend along the way.
And if you are agreed to those conditions,
Tell me at once, without more discussion,
And I will plan to rise early tomorrow to be ready to start."
This thing was granted, and we pledged agreement to his terms
With very glad hearts, and we prayed him also
That he would consent play his part,
And that he would be our governor,
And judge and score keeper of our tales,
And set a supper at a certain price,
And we would abide by his rules
In all things; and thus unanimously
We accepted his authority.
And, to seal the agreement, the wine was fetched immediately;
We drank, and each one of us went to rest,
Without tarrying any longer.
(771-823 Author's modernization)

If we accept that the company consists of twenty-nine (including the Pilgrim, but not including the Host), then Harry Bailey's plan envisages at total of one hundred and sixteen stories. The Host will judge the contest and thus he is the only one of the group whose motivation for making the journey has nothing at all to do with pilgrimage - though it may have a lot to do with his good business sense, his evident ego, and (we learn much later) a desire to get away from his nagging wife.

Given that he was about forty years of age when he began *The Canterbury Tales* in the early 1380s, Chaucer must have though himself capable of writing so much, but in fact he only completed twenty-four of the stories before he abandoned the work. The completed tales exist in various manuscript copies, but the order of the tales is uncertain, and the links between them, which develop the frame story of the journey to Canterbury and the interactions of the pilgrims, are incomplete.

Chapter 2: "Wel nine and twenty in a compaignie"

Introducing the Pilgrims

The dramatis personae, the "nine and twenty in a compaignie, / Of sundry folk" (24-5), do not span the whole range of Chaucer's society. None of the pilgrims comes from the aristocracy, or even the middle nobility, and none comes from the landless, laboring class. Brewer explains Chaucer's focus on this subset of society thus, "The great were too powerful to be represented, the humble were too remote from Chaucer's imaginative experience" (199).

Feudal society was traditionally divided into three estates: the First Estate, the Clergy, who prayed; the Second Estate, the Nobility, who fought; and the Third Estate, the Peasantry, who labored. Such a simplistic tripartite structure, however, increasingly failed to capture the shifting gradations of English society in the late fourteenth century as the rise of an urban merchant class and of a class of university-educated intellectuals (nominally clergy but employed in secular careers), together with a peasant class demanding higher wages and greater freedom, began to break down traditional estate divisions. Gies and Gies describe the erosion of medieval feudal structures in the High Middle Ages:

> [T]he real enemy of the castle barons and their privileges was not the royal power but the slow, irresistible surge of economic change. The cloth merchants and other business men who exploited their workers, not perhaps more brutally, but more effectively than the barons did their villeins, were moving ahead in the economic race… (Gies and Gies 30)

Although accurately categorizing the pilgrims proves difficult, at least ten (the Merchant, the Five Guildsmen, the Cook, the Shipman, the Doctor, and the Wife of Bath) are representative of this new bourgeois, a class of entrepreneurs whose status depends not upon birth or the filling of traditional positions but on their individual skills in their chosen trade or profession. Although Chaucer is frequently contrasted with his contemporaries Gower and Langland who address contemporary social conditions much more directly at a time when social and religious institutions and values appeared to be collapsing, it is precisely this 'middle class' population surge which Chaucer captures in *The Canterbury Tales*.

Whilst the Chaucer-narrator promises confidently to place each pilgrim in his or her "degree," or rank and place in society (40), and in his or her "estaat," or social category (718), it is not surprising that he seems concerned at the end of *The General Prologue* that he has not met this obligation :

> Also, I pray that you will forgive me,
> If I have not set folk in their proper social rank
> Here in this tale, as they should stand.
> My intelligence is limited, you understand.
> (745-748 Author's modernization)

The narrator's concern is understandable since the pilgrims whom he sets out to classify no longer exist in "an archaic and closed social order but [one] that ... reveals that order in the process of breaking down. Most of Chaucer's pilgrims are by no means content to stay in their proper places but are engaged in the pursuit of wealth, status, and respectability" ("Medieval Estates and Orders"). The decline of feudalism was accompanied by the growth of a money-based economy which presented new opportunities for social advancement to the ambitious and the talented.

English society in the second half of the fourteenth century was thus in a constant state of flux. Even the social status of the individual pilgrims is not easy to identify, and critics disagree how they should be defined by status. The following classification is my own:

Minor nobility:	Knight and Squire
Higher clergy:	Prioress and Monk
Lower clergy:	Second Nun, Nun's Priest, Friar and Parson
Church employees:	Pardoner and Summoner (who may be either laymen or in minor orders)
Landed gentry:	Franklin
Professional class:	Clerk, Sergeant of the Law, Doctor
Urban bourgeoisie:	Haberdasher, Carpenter, Webbe, Dyer, Tapicer, Manciple, Harry Bailey
Mercantile class:	Merchant, Shipman, Wife of Bath, and Cook
Rural freemen:	Miller, Reeve
Freemen laborers:	Yeoman, Plowman

The historical Chaucer would fit into the professional class, but the status of the narrator is kept deliberately vague.

The Pilgrims: Types or Individuals?

It was the critic Kittredge who, in 1914, advanced the view that *The Canterbury Tales* should be read as a dramatic poem with fully developed characters and a degree of realism not far removed from that of the modern novel. That Kittredge overstated his case is now generally agreed, for Chaucer left his work unfinished and inconsistent both in its development of individual characters and in the matching of pilgrims to tales. Nevertheless, it remains true that the artistic conception of the *Tales* was something entirely new in medieval literature and that the effort to individualize the pilgrims was an important element of its newness.

Kittredge stresses the realism of the *Prologue* stating confidently:

> There is not one chance in a hundred that he [Chaucer] had not gone on a Canterbury pilgrimage himself. And pilgrims did, for a fact, while away the time in story-telling. (149)

Brewer, reminds us that, "London was a small town, the court of Westminster of course even smaller, and so many of these characters are specific to well-known places there with limited personnel," and argues that, "Chaucer and his primary audience ... were a well-knit group" which would have encouraged the author to include portraits of individuals well known to both (199).

Writing in 1924, Manly notes the "imperfectly schematic" nature of the *General Prologue* (73) and concludes not, as modern detractors tend to assume, "that Chaucer merely described an actual group of pilgrims of which he himself was a member" (70), but that he includes in his fictional account "some at least of the pilgrims [who] were real persons, and persons with whom Chaucer can be shown to have had definite personal contacts" (73). Manly argues that Chaucer was not writing for posterity but for a small audience of nobility and gentry who would have recognized the individuals upon whom most portraits are based and "caught every sly reference to persons and things they knew" (76). Manly concludes that, since Chaucer draws upon his observation of the society of his time, then "Chaucer's character sketches represent not so much types as individuals – typical no doubt of their status and occupations, but typical only as the happily chosen individual may be" (74).

It is fair to say that both the dramatic interpretation and the effort to identify Chaucer's pilgrims with actual historical figures have been passé in literary criticism for some decades now. In the end, we can simply never know if a particular portrait is based on a historical individual, and we may doubt what knowing would actually add to our understanding of the text. In any event, no writer has (so far as I am aware) suggested a historical personage as the basis for the character of the Wife of Bath, though of all of the pilgrims she is the most individualized. Thus, for example, in *The General Prologue* we are told in an apparently throw-away comment that it is a pity that she is a little deaf, but it is only in her own *Prologue* that we learn the full history behind this handicap.

In 1973, reacting against both the dramatic and the historical approaches, critic Jill Mann argued that the *Prologue* belongs to the genre of medieval estates satire, works which attack the abuses and corruptions within the three traditional estates. Mann writes, "Chaucer was concerned to impose an estates form on the *Prologue* in order to suggest society as a whole by way of his representative company of individuals," and that "the estates type was the basis for Chaucer's creation of the Canterbury pilgrims" (in Patterson ed. 26 & 32). The Norton Anthology gives the following account of two examples of estates satire each by a contemporary of Chaucer:

> John Gower's *Mirour de l'Omme* and *Vox Clamantis* systematically indict every estate, order, and profession. They set forth the functions and duties of each estate and castigate the failure of the estates in the present world to live up to their divinely assigned social roles. Unlike their virtuous predecessors in the past, the estates were pursuing wealth, power, and luxury. Although Gower says that his condemnations are aimed only at vicious and not at virtuous persons - and they will know who they are - his presentation of present-day estates is almost uniformly negative.

This helps us to identify that which is traditional and that which is truly original in *The General Prologue*. Chaucer uses the traditional classifications: there is *one* pilgrim for each estate (one Knight, one Pardoner, one Parson, etc.), and each portrait is named for the estate and not for the name of the individual, even though some pilgrims are named. Thus, the Wife of Bath represents secular women who have achieved a certain legal and economic autonomy, yet she is given the distinctive name, Alison, and a number of personality traits which have nothing to do with her estate and everything to do with her personality (a modern reader would say her psychology) and her individual life-experiences.

The Order of the Portraits

In terms of arrangement of his portraits in *The General Prologue*, Chaucer ignores the norm in estates satire that all clerical figures should come before all lay figures and that all men should come before all women. Neither does Chaucer simply substitute a hierarchy based on status for a hierarchy based on literary precedent. It is true that the portraits show a general decline in status from the minor nobility to the freemen, but anomalies are introduced by the arrangement of the pilgrims into small social subsets, which furthers the fiction of  the pilgrims having a real existence. Thus the description of the Yeoman follows that of the Knight and the Squire because he is travelling as part of the Knight's retinue, though in terms of status he is amongst he lowest of the pilgrims, and the Ploughman is included with the Parson, layman alongside cleric, because they are brothers travelling together.

Many critics have sought to rationalize the order of the portraits in the *Prologue*, but no theory has proved convincing, so we may suspect that the lack of order is precisely Chaucer's point. Mann, who insists that the content of the portraits is based on stereotypes and largely embodies the ideas and world-view which are typical of each pilgrim's place in society, nevertheless concludes, "The strict order of estates literature is governed by the notion of function, of hierarchy in a model whose working is divinely established. It is precisely this notion of function that ... Chaucer discards" (Patterson 26). Similarly, Leicester states that "one of the principal themes [of the *Prologue*] is the insufficiency of traditional social and moral classifying schemes – estates, hierarchies, and the like – to deal with the complexity of individuals and their relations" (George 94).

The portrait of the Wife of Bath in the *General Prologue* occurs in a group which contains descriptions of the Five Guildsmen (a Haberdasher, Carpenter, Weaver, Dyer and Tapestry-maker) and their wives (who are not present on the pilgrimage), the Cook, the Shipman, and the Doctor. These all represent the new urban middle class, those who, by their skills and training, are well positioned to make money. Of the group, only the Doctor would have necessarily been born into the prosperous middle class for his years of study at the university would have been expensive. All of the others could have 'worked their way up' to their present position in society (like their contemporary Dick Wittington [c. 1354–1423], thrice Lord Mayor of London). Alison's occupation as a weaver is used in her portrait to establish her economic independence and her arrogant self-confidence, but having been used for this purpose it is never mentioned again.

Conclusions

This is what Chaucer does that no writer of estates satire had ever done before: he gives some of his characters names, indicates where they live, and describes them in terms of character traits, physical appearance and dress in ways which sometimes appear to have no relationship to their estate stereotype. It would be naïve to believe that in doing so he did not base some details upon people who he actually knew.

Chaucer develops the individual personalities of the pilgrims hinted at in the *Prologue* as they interact on their way towards Canterbury, particularly in the exchanges between them when the pilgrims stop to rest and water the horses; and he makes them narrators of stories in which the reader (sometimes) hears their individual voices. Indeed, the careful reader even hears the voices of some of the pilgrims themselves in the descriptions given by the narrator in the *Prologue*.

No doubt Benson is wise to warn against seeing Chaucer as a 'modern' writer and the pilgrims, both as they are initially described and as they develop and interact, "as fully developed and psychologically complex characters, like those we know from a realistic novel or film" (Boitani and Mann 130). Benson reiterates that the descriptions are based on types found in estates satires; that Chaucer's individualization is limited to "insinuations" which create "the illusion of life-like individuality" (in Boitani and Mann 130); and that there are a number of inconsistencies between the way characters are initially described and what we subsequently learn of them. Nevertheless, the fact that Chaucer does not individualize his pilgrim-narrators with the consistency of a modern novelist does not mean that he does not individualize them to a degree quite new in literature.

Chapter 3: The Wife of Bath in *The General Prologue*

The Socio-Economic Context

In 1347, England exported 30,000 sacks of wool and 4,422 cloths, but the average for the years 1392-5 was 19,000 sacks and 43,000 cloths. The reason for the change was that in 1375 the Crown levied a tax of 33% on exports of raw wool and only 2% on finished cloth. The tax was designed to increase the quality and the amount of domestic cloth production. To further this end, Hussey states that "Flemish workers were encouraged to immigrate, and English workers to improve their skill. (Hussey et al. 39)

Howard places the portrait of the Wife of Bath (later identified as "Dame Alisoun") in its socio-historical context:

> Of all the 'middle-class' members, the Wife, a cloth-maker, ranks lowest; where the wives of the Guildsmen aspire to walk at the head of a procession in a 'mantel royalliche ybore,' she is content with (but insisted on) going up first to the offering in her parish church. (96)

Women were, of course, born into one of the Three Estates, but women also had a separate and more significant classification. Based entirely on their relationship with men, they were classed as either: a virgin, a wife, or a widow. Alison is a widow who has buried five husbands, in the process accumulating wealth and raising her social status considerably. She wears a wimple to symbolize her status as a married woman. However, as a widow, she is in the strongest position a medieval woman could be in: she legally owns property in her own right.

Chaucer the Pilgrim and Chaucer the Poet

Those readers who have studied *The General Prologue* will be familiar with the distinction which most critics make between the viewpoints of the narrator-pilgrim and of the poet: it is fundamental to understanding the comedy of the portraits.

The first-person narrator is identified as Geoffrey Chaucer, but this persona is not to be confused with the historical Chaucer, who had a position in the royal administration at court and who is the actual author of *The Canterbury Tales*. The distinction between the Pilgrim and the Poet was first proposed by the critic Donaldson writing in 1954; he defined the Pilgrim as a narrator acutely *unaware* of the real significance of what he observes and records so precisely. This is to say that the character of the Pilgrim, though it borrows aspects of the history, personality, and even physical appearance of the historical Chaucer, is actually as much a literary creation as are the other pilgrims, some of whom are similarly based to some degree on real individuals.

Chaucer the Poet not only has great fun re-inventing himself as a naive observer who takes each of the pilgrims at face value and is mightily impressed by everyone he meets, but also takes delight in using the over-voice of the Poet to inject into the portraits ironic details which undercut his narrator's extravagant praise. This use of dual perspective allows the Poet to exploit the obvious distance in most of the portraits between the enthusiastic praise and admiration of the Pilgrim and the darker reality of the character being described. New Criticism terms the Pilgrim an 'unreliable narrator'.

The Portrait of the Wife of Bath

Study Questions:

The Pilgrim's Perspective:

1. This larger-than-life character really impresses the Pilgrim. What details does he give in praise of: a) Her skills as a weaver; b) Her clothing; c) The way she interacts socially with the other pilgrims?
2. One outstanding feature of this character is the number and variety of pilgrimages she has been on. List the places she has visited and give brief details of their religious significance.

The Poet's Perspective:

Once again, it is the moral failings of the character which the Poet attacks.
1. The adjectives "good" (447) and "worthy" (461) sound like moral approval, but what did these words actually mean in Chaucer's time?
2. The Wife's religious devotion (implied by her enthusiasm for pilgrimages) is seriously undercut by her unchristian behavior when making the offering at Mass. Explain.

3. By now, the reader can see that the Wife is competitive in everything she does – aggressively so. What details of her clothes and her accessories are inserted by the Poet to reinforce this point?

4. Although middle-aged, the Wife has obviously been sexually active (perhaps even hyperactive) for most of her adult life:

a) What physical features indicate her passionate nature?

b) What exactly is implied by the statement that, as well as five husbands, she had "oother compaignye in youth" (463)?

c) At first reading, the line "she koude muchel of wandringe by the weye" (469) appears to refer to the Wife being much-travelled. Explain the deeper, moral meaning intended by the Poet.

> A wealthy widow there was from near Bath,
> But she was a little deaf and that was a pity.
> At weaving she had such skill,
> That she was better than the cloth-makers of Ypres and Gaunt.
> In the whole parish, there was no woman
> Who she allowed to go to the alms-offering in front of her;
> And if any of them did do so then she was so angry
> That she was out of all charity for them.
> Her head-cloths were of very fine material;
> I dare swear that they weighed ten pounds,
> That is the ones she wore on her head on Sundays.
> Her stockings were of a fine scarlet red
> Tightly fastened, and her shoes made of supple new leather.
> Bold was her face and attractive and of a ruddy complexion.
> She was an admirable woman all of her life:
> She had married five husbands at the church door
> Without mentioning other 'boyfriends' she had had when she was young –
> But we do not need to speak about that at present.
> She had been to Jerusalem three times,
> She had crossed many a foreign river;
> She had been to Rome, and Boulogne,
> At the shrine of St. James in Galicia (northwest Spain), and at Cologne.
> She knew a lot about wandering by the wayside.
> Gap-toothed she was, to tell you the truth.
> Upon a walking horse she sat,
> Her forehead covered by a wimple and a hat on her head
> Which was as big as a buckler or a shield;
> She wore an overskirt around her large hips,
> And on her feet a pair of sharp spurs.

In company she laughed and chatted a lot,
She knew the cures for lovesickness without a doubt,
About love she knew all the tricks of the trade.
(447-475 Author's modernization)

The Portrait Analyzed

Like every other pilgrim, this character is introduced by role and status (she is an independently wealthy widow) immediately suggesting that she is a type not an individual. However, whilst there were tens of thousands of knights, squires, friars, monks, etc. in England in Chaucer's day, so that composites could be generalized, there can have been very few women indeed who had achieved independent wealth through multiple remarriage and by being successful in the weaving trade, and still fewer who were from the West Country and called Alison! Thus, it is no surprise that the Wife of Bath has no predecessor in the estates satire literature. The specificity with which she is described in *The General Prologue* and in her own *Prologue,* and the high level of consistency between the two accounts, marks her as a character in the modern sense of that term rather than a type.

Two features combine to define Alison's character. Firstly, in everything she does (be it cloth-making or making an offering at her local parish church), her combative, assertive nature means that she must be first. Secondly, she likes the company of men and feels no shame in saying that she enjoys sex (apparently both inside and outside of marriage) in an age which found female sexual appetite to be inherently sinful. The Wife of Bath herself recognizes the influence of two planets at her birth in forming her temperament:

> For truly, my nature is entirely controlled by Venus
> In feeling, and my brain is controlled by Mars:
> Venus gave me my vigor, my sexual appetite,
> And Mars gave me my bold assertiveness.
> At my birth, Taurus was my ascendant sign, with Mars therein.
> Alas! Alas! That ever love was sin!'
> (608-13 *The Wife of Bath's Prologue* Author's modernization)

Venus makes her sanguine, a "lover of company, fine clothes, gossip and merriment" (Hussey et al. 168), while Mars makes her choleric, "intemperate, brazen, and bent on conquest, a feminine counterpart of the thick-set Miller" (Ibid. 161). The influence upon the Wife of the planet Mars is best seen in contrasting her character with that of the Prioress who is entirely of a sanguine temperament: where the Prioress is delicate and refined in all that she does, the Wife is immodest and self-assertive. Thus, we have a woman who is disposed both psychologically and economically to remarry upon the death of each husband and for whom each relationship must be a fight for sovereignty, in which she is again at odds with her culture which gave sovereignty exclusively and unquestioningly to the male.

The Pilgrim leaps straight into superlatives to describe the Wife's skill in weaving:

> Of clooth-making she hadde swich an haunt,
> She passed hem of Ypres and of Gaunt. (449-50)

Bath was indeed an important commercial centre of the wool trade, and the local cloth, called Bath Beaver, was known throughout England. As so often, the Pilgrim seems in this portrait to be giving the Wife's version of herself, probably paraphrasing her own words, rather than judging for himself. It is by no means clear from the portrait whether weaving is the Wife's profession (at that time it was still a cottage industry there being no factories) or a part-time occupation. As Brown and Butcher point out, the status which is claimed for the Wife in the above lines makes her "an unusual if not unique figure" for:

> Unmarried women and widows, among the less prosperous, might scrape a living performing low-paid labour in trade or craft, engaging in by-employments, serving as domestic labour in more prosperous households, or by prostitution. Exceptionally, it was possible for single women to trade, by special licence, as a *femme sole* or *sola mercatrix*. (Brown and Butcher 27)

No one but the Wife herself would compare Bath Beaver with the fine woolen cloth produced at Ypres and Ghent which had a Europe-wide reputation for high quality. Hussey offers what is almost certainly the correct interpretation of these lines, "When Chaucer notes that she surpassed 'hem of Ypres and of Gaunt' it is possible that he means alien residents in England at the time, rather than the workers at home in Flanders" (Hussey et al. 39). This certainly sounds more likely, but either way, it is an arrogant and unrealistic boast representing Alison's own valuation of her skills.

The portrait of the Wife of Bath is the only one which offers two detailed descriptions of the character's clothing: her Sunday attire, and what she is wearing on the pilgrimage. More than any other character, her garments illuminate her character. The portrait begins with the Wife's Sunday going to Church clothes:

> Hir coverchiefs ful fine weren of ground;
> I dorste swere they weyeden ten pound
> That on a Sonday weren upon hir heed.
> Hir hosen weren of fyn scarlet reed,

Ful streite yteyd, and shoes ful moiste and newe. (455-9)

Everything about this description implies the ostentatious display of wealth and excess. Even if we assume that the coverchiefs are themselves elaborately ornamented, and that they are arranged on and supported by wire frames, the idea that they might weigh ten pounds is comic hyperbole. Note also the repetition of the superlatives "full" and "fine," the bright red of her stockings, and the combined detail that her shoes are of the finest leather and that they are new. The red of the hose which she wears immediately suggests her passionate nature; the wearing of red hose was associated with the nobility, so it is also a sign of the Wife dressing above her station. The phrase "scarlet reed" is not redundant repetition (458): it tells us both that her hose is dyed red and that the hose itself is 'escarlate,' a particularly fine and expensive woolen cloth (Shuster).

Every item of the Wife's clothing is aimed to impress upon others her social status – she is even meticulous in ensuring that the back seams of her hose are straight. There is an unlikely parallel between the Prioress and Alison in that each appears to "countrefete" (139) the behavior of the social class to which they aspire, but into which they were not born, the Wife having gained status and wealth by each successive marriages which perhaps accounts for Alison's aggressive self-assertion in being the first to the offering.

The contrast between the Alison's Sunday best and her pilgrimage clothes could hardly be greater:

Ywimpled wel, and on hir heed an hat …
A foot-mantel aboute hir hipes large, (472-4)

The keynote here is practicality, reminding us that the Wife is a seasoned traveler. She wears a wide-brimmed hat to protect her face from the elements. A wimple serves the same purpose, even at the expense of hiding her forehead, and she wears an overskirt to protect her gown (Shuster). These clothes much more realistically reflect the Wife's true position in society.

The Wife is conventionally religious and makes regular offerings to the Church on Sundays. She has been on pilgrimages to holy places throughout Europe:

And thries hadde she been at Jerusalem;
She hadde passed many a straunge strem;
At Rome she hadde been, and at Boloigne,
In Galice at Seint-Jame, and at Coloigne. (465-8)

The Pilgrim uses this impressive list to suggest a high level of devotion, but the Poet would have the reader see the Wife as a serial palmer (i.e. pilgrim), one whose motives for undertaking a pilgrimage are recreational rather than religious for he describes her as sociable and good company, "In felaweshipe wel koude she laughe and carpe" (476). Her extensive travels also indicate both Alison's financial independence and her self-assurance, for such travel was very expensive and involved a significant degree of person risk.

The first adjective used in this portrait is "good" (447) which coincidentally is the first adjective used to describe the very next pilgrim, the Parson. The difference in meaning is dictated by the context in which the words are used: whilst the Parson is "good" in the moral sense, the same word here simply indicates that the Wife is the mistress of her own house and therefore has a high standing in the town. This same point is re-enforced later in the portrait when we are told:

> She was a worthy womman al hir live:
> Housbondes at chirche dore she hadde five, (461-2)

The Poet's irony here works by juxtaposing what appears to be an approving moral judgment with a detail which undercuts it. As the Wife will explain in her *Prologue*, there were those in the Church who found the notion of a widow remarrying to be a sin. The word "worthy" carries no hint of moral approval; this woman's relatively high social status (literally her worth in monetary terms) and her financial independence is seen to rest on having buried husbands and inherited their estates and not upon her conduct.

The Pilgrim's sharp eye for detail allows the Poet to make it clear that the Wife's sexual morality is extremely suspect. She has married five husbands and been widowed five times. (We learn later in her *Prologue* that she married the first four men because they were rich and old and only the last for love.) These marriages have been conducted, as was the custom for a woman of her class, "at chirche dore" (462):

> [C]ouples usually spoke their vows at the church door, the most public place in the village. Here the priest inquired if there was any impediment, meaning kinship in the degree forbidden by the Church. The bridegroom named the dower which he would provide for his wife, giving her as a token a ring … Vows were then exchanged, and the bridal party might proceed into the church where a nuptial Mass was celebrated. (Gies and Gies 177)

There are clear hints, however, of extra-marital affairs during her first marriage and of subsequent infidelity. The Pilgrim speaks euphemistically of "oother compaignye in youthe" (463), a detail which he simply attempts to skate past, "therof [I] nedeth nat to speke as nowthe" (464). Ironically, the very lengths to which the Pilgrim is forced to go in his effort to minimize the implications of what he says has the effect of drawing them to the reader's attention. Promiscuity is also suggested by such details as:

> She hadde passed many a straunge strem …
> She koude muchel of wandringe by the weye.
> Gat-tothed was she, soothly for to seye. (466-70)

The first two lines are intended by the Pilgrim to relate to the Wife's extensive experience of religious travels throughout Europe, but the Poet intends a metaphorical interpretation: the Wife finds it hard to stick to the straight and narrow path of salvation. The Medieval reader would immediately think of Mathew 7:13-4, "Enter ye in at the strait gate: for wide is the gate, and broad is the way, that leadeth to destruction, and many there be which go in threat: Because strait is the gate, and narrow is the way, which leadeth unto life, and few there be that find it" (King James).

The detail of the gap between her front teeth, which the Pilgrim records as adding to her attraction, complements the previous line, for physiognomy saw being gap-toothed as a sign of a bold nature given to aggressive, wanton and immoral behavior, uncontrolled appetites, lust, and hyper-sexuality. It has been suggested that the very first hint of this aspect of the Wife's character is given in the innocuous-sounding line, "Of clooth-making she hadde swich an haunt," (449). The word "haunt" means 'skill,' but it also means a 'much frequented place' which, in terms of her sexual history, is a pretty good description of Alison.

The Wife's dominant characteristic is her assertiveness. She rides upon an "ambler" (471), that is a palfrey, the most expensive and highly-bred type of riding horse of the Middle Ages, proving once again her affluence. The palfrey was the preferred choice of nobles, knights and ladies for long journeys because its gait provided a smooth and comfortable ride which accounts for the detail that the Wife sat her mount "esily" (471). This being so, it is entirely superfluous that the she wears "on hir feet a paire of spores sharpe" (475). The Poet is highlighting that the Wife must be in control in all situations. The Ellesmere illustration shows her with an equally superfluous whip in her hand, which is not described in the portrait. However, later she will tell the company:

> … when I have told you the rest of my tale
> Of the suffering in marriage
> (Of which I have been an expert all my life
> This is to say, myself have been the whip)
> (173-6 *The Wife of Bath's Prologue* Author's modernization)

She claims to have literally had the whip hand in her marriages.

The Wife wears a wimple, as befits her status as a widow, but one suspects that the adverb "wel" implies that her wimple is as ornate and flattering as is that of the Prioress. She is:

> Ywimpled wel, and on hir heed an hat
> As brood as is a bokeler or a targe; (472-3)

Impressed by the size of the Wife's hat, a simile springs innocently to the pen of the Pilgrim: to him it emphasizes only the immense size of the Wife's hat, but to the Poet it is another indication of her assertive, combative character. John Clements explains the place of the "bokeler" in medieval combat:

> A buckler differs from a shield in that the latter is carried by straps and worn on the arm whereas the former is held in single-hand in a "fist" grip. It is difficult to trace the history of the weapon as many times any type of round shield or small targe would be called buckler, regardless of whether it was held in the fist or worn on the arm. The buckler was a small, maneuverable, hand-held shield for deflecting and punching blows ... Bucklers were typically round and frequently between 8 to 16 inches in diameter.

The second comparison is even more significant since a "targe" was a larger round shield, generally between eighteen and twenty-one inches, usually attached to the forearm.

The Wife's martial spirit is initially shown, most inappropriately, in her determination to be the first to reach the altar with her offering at Mass:

> In al the parisshe wif ne was ther noon
> That to the offringe bifore hire sholde goon;
> And if ther dide, certeyn so wrooth was she,
> That she was out of alle charitee. (451-4)

The Pilgrim presents this detailed description without comment, the unspoken implication being that, like her many pilgrimages, it is another indication of her devotion. The Poet, however, relies upon the reader to understand that being first to the altar was reserved for the person with the highest social position, and that the Wife is merely asserting her worthiness in its purely social sense. This point is hammered home by the comment that if she is beaten by another lady she is furious ("wroth") and full of hard thoughts against her rival ("out of alle charitee"). Wrath is, of course, one of the Seven Deadly Sins and charity one of the Seven Heavenly Virtues.

The final detail which fits into the pattern of the Wife's assertiveness is the Pilgrim's sympathetic remark that "she was somdel deef, and that was scathe" (448). It is later revealed in her *Prologue* that she is deaf in one ear because, during an argument over the relative position of men and women in marriage, her last husband hit her on the side of her head knocking her to the floor. However, at this point in the *General Prologue*, the reader may speculate that her deafness is more psychological than it is physical: the Wife of Bath only hears what she wishes to hear.

In contrast to the detail given in describing the Wife's clothes and her conduct, surprisingly little physical description is given and the details are spread throughout the portrait:

> Boold was hir face, and fair, and reed of hewe. (460)
> Gat-tothed was she, soothly for to seye. (470)
> A foot-mantel aboute hir hipes large, (474)

The Pilgrim finds the Wife physically attractive commenting on her ruddy complexion, the gap between her front teeth and her large hips. Everything points to someone who has been sexually active, and who puts her experience to good use:

> Of remedies of love she knew per chaunce,
> For she koude of that art the olde daunce. (477-8)

Kirkham and Allen gloss her knowledge of remedies as "aphrodisiacs and seduction techniques" (52). This makes even clearer the irony of the fact that she remains childless.

Ladies (by their dress quite wealthy - note the crown!) carding, spinning and weaving. (Engraving 1891 based on a medieval painting. Wikimedia Commons. Public domain.)

Chapter 4: *The Wife of Bath's Prologue*

Introduction

This chapter contains, side-by-side, the Middle English text and a modernized version of the *Prologue* and the *Tale*.

The Middle English text has been edited to make its meaning as clear as possible. In particular, I have used capitalization, paragraphing and modern punctuation (particularly by cutting down on the number of semi-colons and by using parentheses) to help guide the reader through the narrator's frequent shifts of topic. The Wife of Bath has a tendency to go off at a tangent! Important alternative readings of the Middle English text are placed in brackets.

Opposite the Middle English, you will find a version of the text in contemporary English. Books often refer to such versions as translations, but they really are not since Middle English (unlike the Old English of *Beowulf*) is identifiably the same language as Modern English. To illustrate my point, here are the first three lines of *Beowulf*:

> HWÆT, WE GAR-DEna in geardagum,
> þeodcyninga þrym gefrunon,
> hu ða æþelingas ellen fremedon!

If nothing else, that should make Middle English appear more user-friendly!

The commentary aims to point out significant features of the narrative and to provide the sort of historical, social, literary, and linguistic information that Chaucer assumed his original audience would have, but which a reader today might reasonably be expected not to know.

A Note on Sexual Content

The Wife of Bath's Prologue and *Tale* is a text frequently set for students of high school age, thus posing a problem for teachers because of the explicit references which Alison makes to her various relationships and to the sexual organs and their uses. The editor has a similar problem in explaining particular words.

Like Shakespeare, Chaucer lived in a time when people were not as easily embarrassed about bodily functions as they are now. There was very little privacy in medieval houses!

In my modernization and commentary, I have avoided using some of the more offensive contemporary words to describe parts of the female anatomy and the sexual act, but I have only resorted to euphemism when the Wife of Bath does.

'Experience, though noon auctoritee
Were in this world, is right ynough for me
To speke of wo that is in mariage:
For, lordinges, sith I twelf yeer was of age,
Thonked be God that is eterne on lyve,   5
Housbondes at the chirche dore have I had fyve,
If I so ofte myghte have y-wedded bee,
[For I so ofte have y-wedded bee,]
And alle were worthy men in hir degree.
   'But me was toold, certeyn, nat longe agoon is,
That sithen Crist ne went nevere but onis   10
To wedding, in the Cane of Galilee,
That by that ilk ensample taughte he me,
That I ne sholde wedded be but ones.'

Alison is an independent, assertive woman trapped in a patriarchal
society which denies women the right to control their own lives. As a wife,
and now as a widow, she fights against the misogynist (anti-woman) and
misogamist (anti-marriage) stereotypes of women which are used by men to
justify their tyranny.

The practice of child marriage was relatively common in a time when
there was no minimum age for marriage. All that was required was the
agreement of the parents which was invariably based on financial rather than
personal considerations. The marriage would, however, only have the status
of a legal contract; actual consummation and cohabitation would be delayed
until the girl (in this and most other cases the girl was the younger, a sort of
'trophy bride' for a richer, older man) was mature enough to take on her
duties in both the household and the marriage bed. In the Wife's case, this
would have been about three years.

In late fourteenth century England, people who could not read Latin
(which effectively meant most people) learned the Bible from oral versions
of scriptures (particularly sermons), mystery plays, and religious images.
However, between 1382 and 1395, a number of translations of The *Bible* into
Middle English began to appear. Although history describes the result as *The
Wycliffe Bible*, it was the work of a team of translators, but the man behind
the project was John Wycliffe who believed passionately that "it helpeth
Christian men to study the Gospel in that tongue in which they know best
Christ's sentence." This was a disturbingly revolutionary idea at a time when
the Roman Catholic Church, led by God's representative on earth, the Pope,
claimed the sole right to establish church doctrine. In fact, it was heresy, a
charge which Wycliffe rejected, "You say it is heresy to speak of the Holy

24

'Even if not a single authoritative text on the subject
Had survived from ancient times, experience would certainly be
sufficient to qualify me
To speak about the misery that is in marriage:
For, gentlemen, since I was twelve years old,
Thanks be to God who lives eternally,   5
I have married five husbands at the church door
If I might legally have been married so often,
[For that is how many times I have been married],
And all of them were respectable men in their social rank.
     'But I certainly heard, not so long ago,
That because Christ never went above once   10
To a wedding, in Cana in Galilee,
That by that example he taught me
That I should not be married more than once.'

Scriptures in English. You call me a heretic because I have translated the
Bible into the common tongue of the people." He was called to account
before the Church authorities, but having powerful friends at court he
escaped punishment and died of natural causes. (Forty-four years after his
death, in 1428, Wycliffe's remains were recovered and burnt - the normal
punishment for heresy.) It was the role of laymen to accept and to believe,
and laywomen were officially barred from the study of theology.

Thus, in appropriating clerical discourse, in claiming the right to interpret
the Gospels for herself ("'What that he mente therby, I kan nat seyn'" [20]),
and in attacking traditional teaching on celibacy, Alison associates herself
with the heretical Lollard movement which Wycliffe's work spawned.
Lollards, going against Church authority, advocated the remarriage of
widows - another similarity with the Wife. The Lollards first came under
attack following the Peasants' Revolt of 1381 despite the fact that Wycliffe
and other prominent Lollards opposed the revolt. At the height of the
rebellion, however, one of its leaders, the priest John Ball, preached a sermon
at Blackheath just south of London in which he asked provocatively, "When
Adam delved [digged] and Eve span; who was then the gentleman?" As
Blamires states, the Wife of Bath "treads dangerous ground" (Brown 142).

Line 10 refers to John ii 1-2: "And the third day there was a marriage in
Cana of Galilee; and the mother of Jesus was there: And both Jesus was
called, and his disciples, to the marriage" (King James). This is the famous
occasion when Jesus turned the water into wine, though the Wife makes no
reference to this.

'Lo, hearke eek, which a sharpe word for the nones,
Besyde a welle Jhesus, God and man,   15
Spak in repreeve of the Samaritan.
    "'Thou hast y-had fyve housbondes," quod he,
"And that ilke man, that hath now thee,
Is noght thyn housbonde." Thus seyde he certeyn:
What that he mente therby, I kan nat seyn.   20
But that I axe, why that the fifthe man
Was noon housbonde to the Samaritan?
How manye mighte she have in mariage?
Yet herde I nevere tellen, in myn age,
Upon this nombre deffinicioun.'   25

The Wife refers here to John iv 16-18, as though it has been used by
clerical scholars to argue against remarriage. If so, both they and Alison
mistake its meaning, since Jesus is explicitly referring not to the woman's
fifth husband, but to the man with whom she is living unmarried following
the death of her fifth husband: "Jesus saith unto her, 'Go, call thy husband,
and come hither.' The woman answered and said, 'I have no husband.' Jesus
said unto her, 'Thou hast well said, "I have no husband:" For thou hast had
five husbands; and he whom thou now hast is not thy husband: in that saidst
thou truly'" (King James).

This is the beginning of the Wife's conflation of two entirely different
things: bigamy (being married to two or more people concurrently) and
remarriage following the death of a spouse. She is clearly not the first to
muddy the waters by treating the two as synonymous.

We find such conflation in *Against Jovinian* where St. Jerome addresses
this issue. He accepts that the man with whom the Samaritan woman is
cohabiting is her sixth husband and comments "where there is a succession
of spouses, this one ceased to be her husband, for properly speaking only one
man can be the husband. In the beginning one rib was turned into one wife,
'and the two will be in one flesh' (Gen. 2:24) - not three, not four, for
otherwise there are not two of them, if there are more" (Translated A. G.
Rigg in Kolve & Olson 364-5). St. Jerome goes on to argue that the Flood
was sent to destroy both homicide and bigamy. As further support for his
view that remarriage is simply a form of bigamy, he also refers to St. Paul's
injunctions that no bigamist can be a priest and that no widow who has
married more than one husband can be given charity by the Church "even if
she is old and decrepit and starving" because she is not deserving (translated
A. G. Rigg in Kolve & Olson 365). It is against such a tradition of clerical
teaching that the Wife is in revolt.

'Stop and listen to the sharp words on the topic
That Jesus, God and man, standing beside a well,   15
Spoke to reproach the Samaritan woman.
  '"You have had five husbands," he said,
"And that same man that you are now living with
Is not your husband." That's certainly what he said,
Though what he meant by it, I cannot determine.   20
I ask, however, why the fifth man
Was not legally a husband to the Samaritan?
How many could she have legally married?
In all my life, I have never heard tell
A definitive answer as to the permitted number of husbands'.   25

Medieval couple in bed. (Source unknown. Medieval manuscript.
Public domain.)

'Men may devyne, and glosen up and doun,
But well I woot, expres, withoute lye,
God bad us for to wexe and multiplye:
That gentil text kan I well understonde.
Eke well I woot, he seyde myn housbonde   30
Sholde lete fader and mooder, and take me,
But of no nombre mencion made he,
Of bigamye or of octogamye.
Why sholde men speke of it vileynye?
'Lo, heere the wyse king, daun Salomon.   35
I trowe that he hadde wyves mo than oon
(As wolde to God it leveful were to me
To be refresshed half so ofte as he!),
Which yifte of God hadde he for all hise wyvis!
No man hath swich that in this world alyve is.   40
God woot, this noble king, as to my wit,
The firste night had many a myrie fit
With ech of them, so well was him on lyve!'

Current canon law forbade remarriage even after the death of a spouse;
the devour Christian widow was supposed to become and nun. However, the
Wife finds this contrary to God's clear injunction that man should go forth
and multiply: "And you, be ye fruitful, and multiply; bring forth abundantly
in the earth, and multiply therein" (Genesis ix 7 King James). Ironically,
there is no evidence in *The Canterbury Tales* that the Wife has ever had
children or ever wanted them: the only multiplying she has done concerns
husbands and wealth!

On line 30, the Wife refers to Matthew xix 3-6: "The Pharisees also came
unto him, tempting him, and saying unto him, Is it lawful for a man to put
away his wife for every cause? And he answered and said unto them, Have
ye not read, that he which made them at the beginning made them male and
female, And said, For this cause shall a man leave father and mother, and
shall cleave to his wife: and they twain shall be one flesh? Wherefore they
are no more twain, but one flesh. What therefore God hath joined together,
let not man put asunder" (King James). Her argument is based on the fact
that, at this time, Jesus made no reference to the number of wives a man
might take.

The Wife quotes the example of King Solomon as being a wise man
who, quite definitively, was a bigamist. Her argument, however, completely

'Men may speculate and interpret in every way,
But I know definitively, without a lie,
That God commanded us to grow and multiply:
That excellent text I can understand clearly.
Also, I know well that he said my husband   30
Should leave his father and mother and take to me,
But he made no mention of number,
Of marrying two, or eight times.
Why then should men then speak disapprovingly of it?
        'Consider the example of the wise king Lord Solomon.   35
I know very well that he had more wives than one
(I would to God that it was lawful for me
To be provided with a fresh spouse half so often as was he!)
What a gift from God were all his wives!
No living man has such today.   40
God knows, this noble king, as I understand it,
On the first night had many a joyful tumble in bed
With each new wife, so delightful was his life!'

ignores the criticism of Solomon in 1 Kings xi 1-3: "But king Solomon loved many strange women, together with the daughter of Pharaoh, women of the Moabites, Ammonites, Edomites, Zidonians, and Hittites: Of the nations concerning which the LORD said unto the children of Israel, Ye shall not go in to them, neither shall they come in unto you: for surely they will turn away your heart after their gods: Solomon clave unto these in love. And he had seven hundred wives, princesses, and three hundred concubines: and his wives turned away his heart" (King James). Multiple concurrent marriages (i.e. bigamy), the text clearly states, turned Solomon away from the true faith. All of the examples from *The Bible* which Alison uses to defend her right to remarry are taken from the *Old Testament* - another fact which she conveniently ignores.

'Yblessed be God that I have wedded fyve!
[Of whiche I have pyked out the beste,
Bothe of here nether purs and of here cheste.
Diverse scoles maken parfyt clerkes,
And diverse practyk in many sondry werkes
Maketh the werkman parfyt sekirly.
Of five housbondes scoleiing am I.]
Welcome the sixte whan that evere he shal!   45
For soothe, I wol not kepe me chasst in al;
Whan myn housbande is fro the world ygon,
Som Christen man shal wedde me anon.
For thanne th'Apostle seith that I am free
To wedde, a Goddes half, where it lyketh me.'   50

The lines in brackets, "Of whiche … am I" are not found in all manuscripts and may not be Chaucer's. They do, however, contain a delightfully rude joke about the Wife's selection of her husbands for the contents of both their hanging purses and their chests. Both words, of course, imply her concern for wealth, but the "nether purses" also have a sexual connotation relating to the purse-like bag which contains a man's testicles. Whilst this boast is entirely typical of Alison, it is inconsistent with her description of her first three husbands who she characterizes as too old to perform the sexual act well enough to satisfy her.

The Wife's argument in lines 49-50 relies heavily on St. Paul's First Letter to the Corinthians 6-9 where he states: "But I speak this by permission, and not of commandment. For I would that all men were even as I myself. But every man hath his proper gift of God, one after this manner, and another after that. I say therefore to the unmarried and widows, it is good for them if they abide even as I. But if they cannot contain, let them marry: for it is better to marry than to burn" (King James). Notice how the Wife puts the emphasis on the parts of Paul's statement which support her case.

In his introduction to Theophrastus' *The Golden Book on Marriage*, St. Jerome defends his long list of women from pagan times who held virginity to be an absolute value by asking, "what am I to do when the women of our time attack the apostolic authority of Paul, and, before the funeral of the first husband is finished, start repeating from morning to night the arguments which support a second marriage? Seeing they despise the fidelity which the concept of Christian chastity dictates, let them at least learn chastity from the pagans" (Author's version).

'Blessed be God that I have wedded five!
[I have picked out the very best,
Both for their sexual prowess and for their wealth.
Attending a variety of schools makes for a perfect scholar,
And a variety of practice in a range of work
Certainly makes for the perfect workman.
I have learned by being married to five husbands.]
Welcome the sixth whenever that he shall happen along!   45
For truly, I will not keep myself absolutely chaste;
When my husband is dead and gone,
Some Christian man shall marry me as soon as possible.
For, in such a case, the Apostle Paul decrees that I am free
To marry, in God's name, whoever I choose.'   50

Alison declares proudly that she is on the lookout for another husband - and what better place to find "Som Christen man" with high social status and a large disposable income than on a pilgrimage!

It is against clerics who presume to dictate the rules of marriage that Alison is in revolt. (Cours de philosophie à Paris Grandes chroniques de France, fourteenth century. Wikimedia Commons. Public domain.)

'He seith that to be wedded is no sinne;
"Bet is to be wedded than to brinne."
What rekketh me, thogh folk seye vileynye
Of shrewed Lamech, and his bigamye?
I woot well Abraham was an hooly man,   55
And Jacob, eke, as ferforth as ev'r I kan;
And ech of hem hadde wyves mo than two,
And many another holy man also.
Wher can ye saye [Whanne saugh ye ever], in any manere age,
That hye God defended mariage   60
By word expres? I pray you, telleth me.
Or where comanded he virginitee?
I wot as well as ye, it is no drede,
Th'Apostel, whan he speketh of maydenhede,
He seyde that precept thereof hadde he noon.   65
Men may conseille a womman to be oon,
But conseille is no comandement:
He putte it in oure owene juggement.'

By this point the reader begins to wonder why the Wife is conflating two entirely different things, that is, multiple successive marriages and concurrent bigamy. The answer is that Church theologians have done the same thing in order to extend the clear ruling against bigamy to remarriage.

In *The Bible*, Lamech is the first recorded bigamist and the second murderer (Cain being the first). Genesis 19-23 reads: "Then Lamech took for himself two wives: the name of one *was* Adah, and the name of the second *was* Zillah ... Then Lamech said to his wives: 'Adah and Zillah, hear my voice; Wives of Lamech, listen to my speech! For I have killed a man for wounding me, Even a young man for hurting me'" (King James). Since the Wife cannot argue against the wickedness of Lamech or the implication that it is somehow tied to his being a bigamist, she simply dismisses this example and counter-balances it with the names of bigamists who were presented as holy men.

The reference to St. Paul is to 1 Corinthians vii 1-7: "Now concerning the things whereof ye wrote unto me: It is good for a man not to touch a woman. Nevertheless, to avoid fornication, let every man have his own wife, and let every woman have her own husband ... But I speak this by permission, and not of commandment. For I would that all men were even as I myself ... I say therefore to the unmarried and widows, it is good for them

'Paul said that to be married is no sin,
"It is better is to be wed than to burn with lustful desire."
What do I care if people speak about the evil
Of wicked Lamech, and his bigamy?
I know perfectly well that Abraham was a holy man,   55
And Jacob, also, as far as I can understand;
And each of them had more than two wives,
And many another holy man as well.
Where can you show me in any period whatsoever
That God on high forbade marriage   60
Explicitly? I pray you show it to me.
Or where he commanded virginity?
I know as well as you, it is not in doubt, that
The Apostle Paul, when he spoke of maidenhead,
Said that he had no commandment on the subject.   65
Men may advise a woman to remain a virgin,
But moral guidance is no the same as commandment:
He left it in our own judgment.'

if they abide even as I. But if they cannot contain, let them marry: for it is
better to marry than to burn." The reader can once again see Alison's
selective interpretation of the text.

The less than romantic reality of marriage. A wife and servant at work in the kitchen. (Anonymous: *Kuchemaistrey*, Nuremberg, 1485. Wikimedia Commons. Public domain.)

'For, hadde God comanded maydenhead,
Thanne hadde he dampned wedding with the dede,   70
And, certes, if there were no seed ysowe,
Virginitee, wherof thane sholde it growe?
Poul dorste nat comanden, atte leeste,
A thing of which his maister yaf noon heeste.
The dart is set up for virginitee;   75
Cacche whoso may: who runneth best lat see.
     'But this word is not ta'en of every wight,
But ther as God list give it of his might.
I woot wel that th'Apostel was a mayde,
But, natheless, thogh he wroot and sayde,   80
He wolde that every wight were swich as he,
Al nys but conseil to virginitee.
And for to been a wyf, he yaf me leve
Of indulgence, so nis it no repreve
To wedde me, if that my make dye,   85
Without excepcion of bigamye.
Al were it good no womman for to touche
(He mente as in his bed or in his couche),
For peril is both fyr and tow t'assemble -
Ye know what this ensample may resemble!   90
This is all and som: he heeld virginitee
Moore parfit than wedding in freletee.
(Freletee clepe I, but if that he and she
Wolde leden al hir lyf in chastitee.)'

The Apostle Paul uses the race metaphor in 1 Corinthians ix 24-7: "Know ye not that they which run in a race run all, but one receiveth the prize? So run, that ye may obtain. And every man that striveth for the mastery is temperate in all things. Now they do it to obtain a corruptible crown; but we are incorruptible. I therefore so run, not as uncertainly; so fight I, not as one that beateth the air: But I keep under my body, and bring it into subjection: lest that by any means, when I have preached to others, I myself should be a castaway." (King James). Once again, the Wife ignores the nuances in Paul's statement emphasizing that if the goal is to control bodily urges in order to enter the Kingdom of Heaven, she will not be entering the race.

The Wife is arguing against view of clerics that since virginity is the purest moral state, then any other state must necessarily be impure and

'For, had God commanded keeping the maidenhead intact,
Then he would necessarily have condemned marriage,   70
And certainly, if there were no seed sown
How could virginity ever come into being?
This, at least, is certain: Paul dared not make a commandment
Concerning something on which his master gave no ruling.
The prize is set up for virginity;   75
Win it who ever may. Let's see who runs the fastest.
      'But this guidance is not meant for everybody
But only by those whom it pleases God to give his strength.
I know well enough that Paul the Apostle was a virgin,
But nevertheless, although he wrote and stated that   80
He wished every person was in the same state as he,
All this is only encouragement to virginity.
And since Paul gave me the right to be a wife
By his permission, then it is no shame
For me to marry, if my husband should die,   85
Without incurring the accusation of bigamy.
Ideally, he might be right that it is better for a man not to touch a
woman
(He meant in his bed or on his couch),
Because it is dangerous to bring together fire and flax -
You know what this symbol represents.   90
This is what it all adds up to: Paul held virginity
Morally superior to marrying in moral frailty to indulge one's sexual
desires.
(I call it moral frailty unless the man and the woman both
Lead their lives in total chastity).'

therefore sinful. However, in the view of the Wife, although virginity is the
purest state, it is reserved only for the saintly. Ordinary people may marry
and procreate (and by implication even enjoy doing it!) without being
regarded as sinful. By conceding this point, she later says that hopes that her
views will not anger the clerics - an unrealistic hope!

'I graunte it wel; I have of noon envye,   95
Thogh maydenhede preferre to bigamye;
Hem lyketh to be clene, body and goost.
Of myn estaat, I nyl nat make no boost.
For wel ye knowe, a lord in his houshold
Hath not every vessel al of gold;   100
Somme been of tree, and doon hir lord servyse.
God clepeth folk to him in sondry wyse,
And everich hath of God a proper yifte:
Som this, som that, as lyketh him to shifte.

  'Virginitee is greet perfeccioun,   105
And continence eke with devocioun,
But Crist, that of perfeccioun is the welle,
Bade nat every wight he shoulde go selle
All that he had, and yeve it to the poore,
And in such wyse folwe him and his foore.   110
He spake to them that would live parfitly,
And, lordinges, by your leve, that am nat I!
I wol bestowe the flour of al myn age
In the acts and in the fruyts of mariage.'

The Wife's use of the metaphor of utensils in a lord's house being of a variety of materials seems powerful, but it is not the interpretation given by St. Paul in 2 Timothy ii 20-3: "But in a great house there are not only vessels of gold and of silver, but also of wood and of earth; and some to honour, and some to dishonour. If a man therefore purge himself from these, he shall be a vessel unto honour, sanctified, and meet for the master's use, and prepared unto every good work. Flee also youthful lusts: but follow righteousness, faith, charity, peace, with them that call on the Lord out of a pure heart" (King James). Paul stresses that every man should endeavor to become a vessel made of pure material in order to serve his Lord with honor. In contrast, Alison's argument is that God made her the way she is, so she will live according to her nature and not try to change it.

In lines 102-4, the Wife more correctly paraphrases 1 Corinthians vii 7: "For I would that all men were even as I myself. But every man hath his proper gift of God, one after this manner, and another after that" (King James) where Paul acknowledges that though virginity is, in his view, preferable, all men are called to God in different ways.

In 1 Corinthians vii 5, Paul urges married couples to have sex together in order to avoid the sinful temptation to be unfaithful. The only exception he

'I freely accept, without any resentment,   95
That remaining single is morally superior to remarrying
For those it pleases to be pure in body and spirit.
Of my own moral standing, I do not boast.
But you know very well that a lord in his household
Does not have every utensil made out of gold;   100
Some are of wood, and yet they do their lord good service.
God calls people to him in various ways,
And each one hath from God his own proper nature:
Some this, some that, as he has been pleased to ordain it.
    'Virginity is great perfection,   105
As is sexual abstinence when combined with religious devotion,
But Christ, who is the fountainhead of perfection,
Did not command that every one should go sell
All that he had, and give it to the poor,
And in such wise follow him and his example.   110
He spoke to those who would live perfectly'
And gentlemen, by your leave, I am not one such!
I will give the prime of my life
In the experience and the pleasures of marriage.'

allows is when couples consent to abstain from sex in order to concentrate on their religious devotions: "Defraud ye not one the other, except it be with consent for a time, that ye may give yourselves to fasting and prayer; and come together again, that Satan tempt you not for your incontinency" (King James).

The assertion that Christ did not tell everyone that they should sell all they have and give the proceeds to the poor refers to the account of the young man, in Matthew xix 21, who asked Jesus what things he should do to attain eternal life: "Jesus said unto him, If thou wilt be perfect, go *and* sell that thou hast, and give to the poor, and thou shalt have treasure in heaven: and come *and* follow me" (King James). Once again, the Wife is strictly speaking correct: Jesus does not say everyone must do this, but he *does* say that everyone who wants to go to Heaven must do so.

Alison refers to bestowing "the flour of al myn age" in marriage. At the time of the pilgrimage, however, the Wife is in her mid-forties, and later she will acknowledge this in a poignant statement which plays upon the flower/flour pun in line 113, "The flour is goon; ther is namoore to telle: / The bren, as I best kan, now moste I selle" (477-8). It is in such humanizing moments that the Wife of Bath comes alive to the reader.

'Tell me also, to what conclusioun   115
Were membres maad of generacioun,
And of so parfit wys a wight y-wroght?
Trusteth me right wel, they were nat maad for noght.
Glose whoso wole, and seye bothe up and doun,
That they were maked for the purgacioun   120
Of urine, and our bothe thinges smale,
And eke to knowe a femele from a male,
And for noon oother cause - sey ye no?
Experience woot well it is noght so.
So that the clerkes be nat with me wrothe,   125
I say this: that they ben maked for bothe,
That is to seye, for office, and for ese
Of engendrure, ther we nat God displese.
Why sholde men elles in hir bookes sette,
That man shall yelde unto his wyf hire dette?   130
Now wherwith sholde he make his payement,
If he ne used his sely instrument?
Thanne were they maad upon a creature
To purge uryne, and eke for engendrure.'

The Wife gives a medieval biology/theology lesson. Her conclusion is simple: God would not have given man organs designed both to purge waste and to reproduce had he not intended man to use those organs for *both* functions. This being so, it is clear to Alison that God intended humans to take pleasure in the act of procreation.

In his *Against Jovinian*, St. Jerome addresses this issue. His argument is that if we are in this way to justify the use of the genitals for procreation then we reduce ourselves to the level of animals: there can be no limit to our lust, no argument for limiting procreation to within marriage, and no objection to adultery. If the genitals are meant for procreation, St. Jerome argues, on what grounds can a man possibly object to his wife being inseminated by another man? In heaven, he continues, men and women will be resurrected bodily in their sex, but, like the angels, they will not perform the offices of sex, and thus those who have remained virgins on earth have already prepared themselves for their resurrected state.

Alison's argument amounts to this: if God put it there, then he must have meant us to use it! She points out that the clerical injunction to chastity is in conflict with the direction that a man must pay his debt to his wife, which the Wife interprets as a reference to sex.

'Tell me also, for what purpose   115
Were the reproductive organs made,
And human beings designed so perfectly?
Trust my word; they were not made for nothing.
Interpret whoever will, and offer all the arguments you like,
For example that they were made for purgation   120
Of urine, and that the small bits that each gender has
Were made simply to differentiate a female from a male,
And for no other cause. Do you deny that this is how clerics argue?
Experience demonstrates clearly that it is not so.
To make sure that the clerics cannot be angry with me,   125
I say this: that they were made for both,
That is to say, for necessary functions and to provide pleasure
During procreation, in which we do not therefore displease God.
Why else should men clearly set down in their books
That a man shall pay his wife her debt?   130
Now with what should he make his payment,
If he does not use his humble tool?
Therefore it is proved that they were they added to the human frame
To discharge urine, and ensure procreation.'

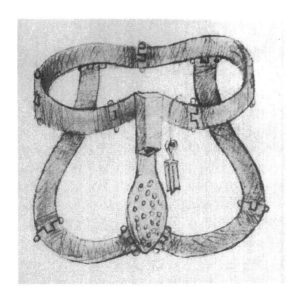

The chastity belt - ultimate male answer to controlling the female sexual impulse. (Manuscript of *Bellifortis* a late 14th-century book on military technology by retired soldier Kyeser von Eichstadt [born 1366]. Wikimedia Commons. Public domain.)

'But I seye nat that every wight is holde,   135
That hath swich harneys as I to yow told,
To goon and usen hem in engendrure:
Thanne sholde men take of chastitee no cure.
Crist was a mayde, and shapen as a man,
And many a seint, sith that this world bigan;   140
Yet ever lyved they in parfit chastitee.
I nyl envye no virginitee:
Let hem be breed of pured whete-seed,
And lat us wyves eat hoten barly-breed.
And yet with barly-breed, Mark telle kan,   145
Oure Lord Jhesu refresshed many a man.'

The reference in lines 145-6 is to Mark vi 33-44 which describes Jesus feeding the five thousand with five loaves and two fishes. Mark, however, does not actually mention the type of bread; reference to barley bread comes in John vi 9. This would seem to be Chaucer's error.

St. Jerome argues that purest wheat bread (which represents virginity) should be the food of choice, but concedes that where starvation reduces the option to eating either cow-dung or barley bread, then barley bread is preferable. He adds, however, that comparing something (barley bread) to something else which is obviously evil (cow-dung) does not establish that the first thing as "good by nature" (*Against Jovinian* Translated A. G. Rigg in Kolve & Olson 361).

There is another play upon the flower/flour pun in line 113. Alison would have known the difference between very expensive fine white bread and the cheaper and courser barley bread, and since she has no vocation for sainthood she is happy to identify with the latter. Various critics have pointed out however, that Alison continually refers to her sex (both the body part itself and the way in which she uses it) in terms of commodities which are bought and sold. Given her life-experiences it would be surprising if she did not.

The Wife, under cover of humility, is making a telling contrast between herself and the misogynistic clerks: unlike them, she is not trying to force her values and her way of life on anyone else, nor is she seeking to denigrate those who live their lives differently.

'But I do not say every person is bound   135
Who has such equipment as I described,
To go and use it to procreate:
In that case men would have no respect for chastity.
Christ was a virgin, yet he was formed as a man,
As was many a saint since the world began;   140
In spite of which, they lived ever in perfect chastity.
I have no quarrel at all with virginity.
Let such people be like bread made from pure white wheat flour,
And let us wives be like barley bread.
And yet with barley-bread, as Mark describes,   145
Jesus fed many a man.'

A mediaeval scholar writing a manuscript at his desk with his quill
pen (a feather trimmed, slitted and used for writing) in his right hand.
(Openclipart. Public domain.)

'In swich estaat as God hath cleped us,
I wol persevere, I nam nat precious.
In wyfhode I wol use myn instrument
As frely as my Makere hath it sent;   150
If I be daungerous, God yeve me sorwe!
Myn housbande shal it have, bothe eve and morwe,
Whan that him list com forth and paye his dette.
    'An housbande wol I have, I nyl nat lette,
Which shal be bothe my debttour and my thral,   155
And have his tribulacioun withal
Upon his flesh, whyle that I am his wyf.
I have the power duringe al my lyf
Upon his propre body, and noght he.
Right thus th'Apostle tolde it unto me,   160
And bade our housbandes for to love us weel;
Al this sentence me lyketh every deel.'

The Wife succeeds in presenting herself as being loyal to God's design in that she will not seek to change anything about the nature which he chose to give her! This entirely ignores all of the scripture that she has just quoted which exhorts man to perfect himself. Her misinterpretation leaves her free to do exactly what she enjoys doing.

The argument moves rather abruptly in lines 155-7 from celebrating sexuality in marriage to the issue of the suffering that is in marriage. The Wife's reference is to 1 Corinthians vii 28: "But and if thou marry, thou hast not sinned; and if a virgin marry, she hath not sinned. Nevertheless such shall have trouble in the flesh: but I spare you" (King James). The wife ignores the plural pronoun in the text and assumes that it is only men who must suffer in marriage, and "the flesh" is, to her, clearly a reference to sex. Similarly she refers to 1 Corinthians vii 2-4: "Nevertheless, to avoid fornication, let every man have his own wife, and let every woman have her own husband. Let the husband render unto the wife due benevolence: and likewise also the wife unto the husband. The wife hath not power of her own body, but the husband: and likewise also the husband hath not power of his own body, but the wife" (King James). Once again, the Wife reads only the part of Paul's pronouncement which fits her of feelings on the relative positions of men and women in marriage, that is, that the man must obey his wife.

'To such condition as God has called us
I will continue; I am not over particular.
Within marriage, I will use my sexual organ
As generously as my Maker bestowed it.   150
If I be fastidious, God give me sorrow!
My husband shall have it both night and day,
Whenever it pleases him to come forth and pay his debt.
   'A husband I will have (I will not leave off)
Who shall be both my debtor and my slave,   155
And have his suffering also
Upon his flesh, while I am his wife.
I have control all my life
Over his own body, not he.
This is just what I learned from Paul the Apostle,   160
Who commanded our husbands to love us well.
This teaching pleases me in every way.'

The marriage vows of men and women were not the same. The man was
asked: "Wilt thou have this Woman to be thy wedded wife, to live together
after God's ordinance in the holy estate of Matrimony? Wilt thou love her,
comfort her, honour, and keep her, in sickness and in health; and forsaking
all other, keep thee only unto her, so long as ye both shall live?" In contrast,
the woman was asked: "Wilt thou have this man to be thy wedded husband,
to live together after God's ordinance in the holy estate of Matrimony? Wilt
thou **obey him**, and **serve him**, love, honour, and keep him in sickness and in
health; and, forsaking all other, keep thee only unto him, so long as ye both
shall live?" The man viwed: "I, ..., take thee, ..., to my wedded wife, to have
and to hold from this day forward, for better for worse, for richer for poorer,
for fairer or fouler, in sickness and in health, to love and to cherish, till death
us depart, according to God's holy ordinance; and thereunto I plight thee my
troth." In contrast, the woman says: "I, ..., take thee, ..., to my wedded
husband, to have and to hold from this day forward, for better for worse, for
richer or poorer, in sickness and in health, **to be bonny and buxom at bed
and at board,** to love and to cherish, till death us depart, according to God's
holy ordinance; and thereunto I plight thee my troth." ("The Form of
Matrimony in the European Middle Ages" As reconstructed by W. J.
Bethancourt III, ULC.)

Up sterte the Pardoner, and that anon.
'Now, Dame,' quod he, 'by God and by Seint John,
Ye been a noble prechour in this cas!   165
I was aboute to wede a wyf, alas!
What? sholde I bye it on my flessh so deere?
Yet hadde I levere wed no wyf to-yeer.'
    'Abyde!' quod she. 'My tale is nat begonne.
Nay, thou shalt drinken of another tonne   170
Ere that I go, shall savoure wors than ale.
And whan that I have told thee forth my tale
Of tribulacioun that is in mariage
(Of which I am expert in al myn age -   175
This is to seyn, myself hath been the whippe),
Then maystow chese whether thou wolt sippe
Of thilke tonne, that I now shal broche.
Be war of it, ere thou to ny approach,
For I shall tellen ensamples mo than ten.   180
"Whoso will nil be war by othere men,
By him shul othere men corrected be."
These same wordes wryteth Ptholomee;
Rede in his *Almageste*, and take it ther.'

After such a long monologue, the sudden interruption of another pilgrim comes as a complete surprise - and, if we are honest, a bit of a relief! It is interesting that the speaker is the Pardoner, for in *The General Prologue* he is described as a very feminine sort of man and there is more than a hint that he is homosexual. (His particular 'friend' is the Summoner.) Either this is one of those inevitable inconsistencies which final revision of the whole work would have corrected, or Chaucer is simply making a point about the Pardoner's need to be the center of attention. At this point, it is impossible to decide.

Apparently the quote on lines 181-2 is not from work cited by Alison, though it is from Ptolemy. This is more likely to be Chaucer's error that the Wife's.

Up jumped the Pardoner suddenly;
'Now, madam,' he said, 'by God and by Saint John!
You are a noble preacher on this subject.   165
Alas, I was about to wed a woman!
But why should I pay for it so dearly on my own flesh?
I had rather marry no wife ever!'
    'Wait!' she said. 'My tale is not begun.
No, you shall drink from a different barrel   170
Before I finish, which shall taste worse than ale.
And when I have told you the rest of my tale
Of the suffering in marriage
(Of which I have been an expert all my life   175
This is to say, myself have been the whip)
Then you may choose whether to take a sip
Of that same barrel that I shall have broken open.
Beware of it, before you get too near;
For I shall give examples more than ten.   180
"Whoever will not be warned by the experience of other men,
Shall be an example by which other men shall be corrected."
Ptolemy writes those words;
Read them in his *Almagest*, and study them there.'

The Pardoner as described in *The General Prologue* (Alfred W. Pollard, *Chaucer's Canterbury Tales: The Prologue*, London: Macmillan (1903). Source: Free EBook, Google Books. Public domain)

'Dame, I wolde praye yow, if youre wil it were,
Seyde this Pardoner, 'as ye bigan,   185
Telle forth youre tale, and spareth for no man,
And teche us yonge men of your praktyke.'

    'Gladly,' quoth she, 'sith that it may yow lyke,
But yet I praye to al this compaignye,
If that I speke after my fantasye,   190
To taketh noght agrief what I seye,
For myne entent nys but for to pleye.

    'Now, sire, then wol I telle you forth my tale.
As evere moot I drinken wyn or ale,
I shal seye sooth: the housbandes that I hadde   195
As thre of hem were goode, and two were badde.
The thre were goode, and riche, and olde
Unnethe mighte they the statut holde
In which that they were bounden unto me.
(Ye wot well what I meene of this, pardee!)   200
As God me help, I laughe when that I thinke
How pitously anight I made hem swinke!
But, by my fey, I tolde of it no stoor.
They had me yeven hir lond and hir tresoor;
Me neded nat do lenger diligence   205
To winne hir love, or doon hem reverence.
They loved me so wel, by God above,
That I ne tolde no deyntee of hir love.'

When she begins the history of her own marriages, Alison moves from a defense of marriage (and hence of remarriage) to a consideration of the position of women within marriage (and by extension in society). Wetherbee explains the prevailing view of woman as "an irrational creature of whim and appetite, constantly in need of the discipline of superior male judgment" (73). Alison offers a critique of the narrow role allowed to women in society and of the misogynist clichés upon which it is based.

The Wife regards her first three husbands as 'good.' From her own account, she would have been in her teens and twenties at the time of her first three marriages, that is, at the very height of her vigor and her beauty. These men were all old, at least by the standards of the day, and because they doted on her, she had no problem in controlling all aspects of these marriages - including sexual relations. Their lack of sexual vitality appears to have been taxed to satisfy Alison in bed.

'Madam, I beg of you, if it is your wish'
The Pardoner said, 'that just as you began   185
You will tell us your tale and do not let any man stop you,
And out of your practical experience teach us younger men.'
    'I'll do so gladly,' said she, 'since it may entertain you,
But first I pray of this company,
If I should speak as my mood may lead me,   190
Not to be upset by what I say,
For my intent is nothing but to pass the time pleasantly.
    'My lords, I now proceed with my tale.
As ever I wish to drink wine or ale in my life,
I shall tell the truth: of the husbands that I have had,   195
Just as three of them were good, two of them were bad.
The three men who were good were rich and old,
Indeed, they were scarcely able to fulfill the [sexual] contract
Of marriage binding them to me.
(You know exactly what I mean by that, I guess!)   200
So help me God, I laugh when I remember
How pitifully I made them toil all night!
Though, by my faith, their suffering did not mean anything to me.
They had given me their land and their money
So I did not need to make any effort   205
To win their love, or show them respect.
They loved me so much, by God above,
That I set no value on their love.'

Her last two husbands were 'bad.' Although by this time she would have
been in her thirties, her fourth husband (who we soon learn kept a mistress)
was certainly the older of the two. He sought to curb her desire to go out and
about to enjoy herself and was (not without justification) jealous of her
flirting with the clerk, Jankin. Nevertheless, ultimately the battle was one-
sided, and the Wife boasts about how she easily got the better of him.

    When she finally married Jankin, Alison was forty and Jankin only
twenty, and for the first time the roles within the marriage were reversed
because she was completely infatuated with him. In addition, it only became
evident after they were married that Jankin's will to power was at least as
strong as her own. The result was a memorable battle for mastery in
marriage.

'A wys womman wol bisye [sette] hire evere in oon
To get hire love, ye, ther as she hath noon.   210
But, sith I hadde hem hoolly in myn hond,
And that they hadde me yeven al hir lond,
What sholde I taken keepe hem for to plese,
But sith it were for my profit, or myn ese?
I sette hem so a-werke, by my fey,   215
That many a night they songen, "Weilawey!"
The bacon was nat fet for hem, I trowe,
That som men han in Essexe, at Dunmowe.
I governed hem so well, after my lawe,
That ech of hem ful blisful was and fawe   220
To bringe me gaye thinges fro the fayre.
They were ful glad whan that I spak hem fayre,
For, God it woot, I chidde hem spitously.
    'Now herkneth hou I baar me proprely.
Ye wys wyves, that kan understonde,   225
Thus shul ye speke and bere hem wrong on honde,
For half so boldely kan ther no man
Swere and lyen as a womman kan.
(I say nat this by wyves that been wyse,
But if it be whan they hem misavyse.)   230
A wys wyfe, if that she kan hir good,
Shall bere hem on hand the cow is wood,
And take witnesse of her owene mayde
Of hir assent: but hearkneth how I sayde.'

A side of bacon was awarded annually at Dunmow in Essex to couples
who claimed not to have quarreled or been unhappy in their marriage for a
year, and who swore that, given the chance, they would choose the same
marriage partner again. It was called the Dunmow Fitch. Later Alison will
state, "yet in bacon hadde I nevere delyt" (418).

Lines 232-234 do not make much sense to the modern reader but would
have caused a medieval reader no problem. They refer to the well known
story of the talking pet bird that tells the husband of his wife's unfaithfulness.
How the wife (who is, of course, guilty) gets out of this fix by persuading the
husband that the bird is insane and calling witnesses to vouch for her
constancy, is to Alison further proof of the superiority of women when it
comes to lying.

48

'A wise woman will constantly busy herself until she has won
The love she wants, particularly where she feels none.   210
But since I had them in the palm of my hand
And they had given to me all of their land,
Why should I give a thought to trying to please them,
Unless it were for my own profit or for my pleasure?
But by my faith, I set them to work for so long   215
That many a night they sang out, "Wo is me!"
The bacon was not brought home for them, I vow,
Like it is for some men at Dunmow in Essex.
I controlled them so strictly by my rules
That each of them was totally happy and anxious   220
To bring me back pretty things from the fair,
And they were delighted when I would speak pleasantly to them,
For God knows I would scolded them bitterly.
     'Now listen to how well I conducted myself.
You prudent women who know what I mean,   225
This is how you should speak, and always keep them in the wrong.
There is no man who can profanely swear and lie
Half as boldly as can a woman.
(I do not say this to those wives who are already prudent,
Except when they have acted imprudently.)   230
If she knows what is good for her, a clever wife
Will make them believe that the talking crow has gone stark mad,
And call as witness her own maid to support her story
By her testimony. Now listen to how I spoke to them.'

An important feature of the *Prologue* is that Alison does not seek to argue against the negative female stereotype constructed by the misogynistic clerics in their texts. Rather, she embraces that stereotype. In her view, women are better liars and swearers than men, and much more cunning. She will later (in her *Tale*) acknowledge that women love flattery, hate to be told their faults, and cannot keep a secret. Alison is not apologizing for her femininity; she is celebrating it.

"'Sire, olde kaynard, is this thyn array?   235
Why is my neighebores wyf so gay?
She is honoured over al ther she gooth,
I sitte at hoom, I have no thrifty clooth.
What dostow at my neighebores hous?
Is she so fair? Artow so amorous?   240
What rowne ye with our mayde? Benedicite!
Sire, olde lechour, lat thy japes be.
And if I have a gossib, or a freend,
Withoute gilt, thou chydest as a feend,
If that I walke or pleye unto his hous.   245
Thou comest home as dronken as a mous,
And prechest on thy bench, with yvel preef.
Thou seyst to me, it is a greet meschief
To wedde a povre woman, for costage,
And if that she be riche, of heigh parage   250
Thanne seistow that it is a tormentrye
To suffre hire pryde and hire malencolye.
And if that she be fair, thou verray knave,
Thou seyst that every holour will hire have;
She may no whyle in chastitee abyde,   255
That is assailled upon ech a side!'"

Compare lines 235-42, with what Theophrastus writes of women, "Then come curtain-lectures, constant grumbling all night. She complains, 'This lady goes out better dressed than me and everyone admires her while I am a poor despised nobody in ladies' company. Why did you ogle that girl next door? Why were you saying to the maid? What did you bring me from the market? I am not allowed to have a single friend, or companion'" (From *The Golden Book of Marriage* Author's version). Notice that the Wife's *Tale* concludes with a curtain lecture but one with a moral intent much different from Theophrastus' stereotype of the nagging, self-obsessed wife.

"'Old Sir Sluggard, is this the way you dress me?   235
Why is my neighbor's wife so finely adorned?
She is so honored everywhere she goes, while
I sit at home because I have no fine clothes.
What are you up to at my neighbor's house?
Is she so beautiful? Are you so highly sexed?   240
What do you whisper with our maid? Bless me!
Old Sir Lecher, stop your dirty tricks!
And if I have a confidant or friend
In all innocence, you chide me like a devil
If I so much as walk or skip to this man's house.   245
You come home just as drunk as a mouse
And preach upon your 'judge's bench'. Bad luck to you!
You say to me that it is a great misfortune
To marry one who is poor because of the expense,
And if she is rich and of good family   250
You say it is sheer torment
Putting up with her pride and moodiness.
And if she is beautiful, you absolute knave,
You say that every lecher will seduce her,
That she will not long remain virtuous   255
When she is assailed on every side.'"

"'Thou seyst som folk desyren us for richesse,
Somme for oure shap, some for oure fairnesse,
And som for she kan outher synge or daunce,
And som for gentillesse and daliaunce,   260
Som for her handes and her armes smale -
Thus goth al to the devel, by thy tale!
Thou seyst, men may nat kepe a castle wal,
It may be so long assailled over al.'"

The word "shap" (258) is a double entendre, that is, "a word or expression that can be understood in two different ways with one way usually referring to sex" (Mirriam-Webster). The word clearly refers to a person's figure, but it also can refer to the genitals of either men or women. This meaning gives much more point to the Wife's statement about the reasons men have for choosing their wives.

Alison's list of the things that (she pretends) her drunken husbands have accused women of, is very similar in style to her list of the answers which the knight receives to his enquiry about what women most desire (see lines 925-48). The resemblance is more, however than the repetition of the word "Some" at the start of the line and the animated nature of the verse. Both are lists of 'qualities' which men ascribe to women and therefore are concerned with negative stereotyping of women. It is part of Chaucer's originality that his imaginative creation, the Wife of Bath, does not concern herself with refuting the female stereotype. Rather, she accepts and unapologetically exalts in it.

'"You say that some desire us for our fortunes,
Some for our looks, some for our beauty,
And some because she can either sing or dance,
Some for her noble blood and flirtatious ways,   260
Some for her delicate hands and arms.
So, according to you, everyone goes to the devil.
You say that men cannot defend a castle wall
That is for so long attacked from all sides."'

Man and woman embracing. (Walters Museum MS W.166, f.16r.
Public domain.)

"And if that she be foul, thou seist that she   265
Coveiteth every man that she may se,
For as a spaynel she wol on him lepe,
Till that she fynde som man her to chepe.
Ne noon so grey goos gooth ther in the lake,
As, seistow, that wool been withoute a make.   270
And seyst, it is a hard thing for to welde
A thing that no man wole, his thankes, helde.
Thus seistow, lorel, whan thou goost to bedde,
And that no wys man nedeth for to wedde,
Ne no man that entendeth unto hevene.   275
With wylde thunder dint and firy levene
Moote thy welked nekke be to-broke!
    "'Thow seyst, that dropping houses, and eke smoke,
And chyding wyves, maken men to flee
Out of his owene house. Ah Benedicitee!   280
What eyleth swich an old man for to chyde?
    "'Thow seyst, we wyves wol oure vyces hyde,
Till we be fast, and thanne we wol hem shewe.
Wel may that be a proverbe of a shrewe.
    "'Thow seyst, that oxen, asses, hors, and houndes,   285
They ben assayed at diverse stoundes,
Bacins, lavours, er that men hem bye,
Spoones, stooles, and all swich housbondrye,
And so been pottes, clothes, and array,
But folk of wyves maken noon assay,   290
Till they be wedded. Olde dotard shrewe!
And thanne, seistow, we wol oure vyces shewe.'"

The accusations come quick and fast. In fact, the husbands would have no time to consider one accusation before being hit by the next - which is, of course, the whole point. The analogy of marriage and buying goods at market brings us very close to the reality of the Wife of Bath's life.

Compare lines 253-6 and 265-70 with Theophrastus, "If a woman be fair, she soon has lovers; if she be ugly, she is herself lustful. It is difficult to guard what many men desire, but it is misery to have what no one thinks worth possessing. However, the misery of having an ugly wife is less than that of keeping watch on a fair one" (From *The Golden Book of Marriage* Author's version).

"'If she looks ugly, then you declare that she   265
Will lust after every man she sees,
And leap on him like a spaniel does
Until she finds a man who will take her.
In all the lake there is not one goose so gray,
You say, that it will be without a mate.   270
And you say it is a hard thing to control
Something that no man willingly would own.
This is how you talk , wretch, when you come to bed,
And that a wise man has no need to marry,
Certainly not any man whose aim is to enter heaven.   275
May a violent clap of thunder and fiery lightning
Come down and break your withered neck!
    "'You say a house that leaks, and also one that gathers smoke,
And wives who scold, cause men to run away
From their own homes. Ah. God bless us!   280
What ails such an old man to chide like this?
    "'You say we wives will hide our vices
Until we are married, and then we let them show.
That's the proverb of a malevolent man!
    "'You say the oxen, asses, horses and hounds,   285
A number of times are closely examined,
As are basins and bowls before a purchase is made,
And spoons and stools, and other household goods
And so are pots, fabrics, and clothing;
But men folk never test their wives,   290
Till they are married (You doddering old rascal!),
And then, you say, we show our vices.'"

Compare lines 282-92 with Theophrastus, "Moreover, in the case of a
wife you cannot choose; you take her as you find her. If she has a bad
temper, is a fool, if she is ugly, or proud, or has bad breath, whatever her
fault may be, we only find it out after marriage. On the other hand, horses,
asses, cattle, even slaves of the smallest worth, clothes, kettles, wooden seats,
cups, and earthenware pitchers, are first tried and then bought; a wife is the
only thing that is not shown before she is married, for fear that her faults will
put off the purchaser" (From *The Golden Book of Marriage* Author's
version).

'"Thou seyst, also, that it displeseth me,
But if that thou wolt preyse my beautee,
And but thou poure alwey upon my face,   295
And clepe me 'faire dame' in every place;
And but thou make a feeste on thilke day
That I was born, and make me fressh and gay;
And but thou do to my norice honour,
And to my chamberere withinne my bour,   300
And to my fadres folk, and his allyes."
Thus sayest thou, old barel-ful of lies.

'"And yet of oure apprentice, Janekyn,
For his crispe heer, shyninge as gold so fyn,
And for he squiereth me bothe up and doun,   305
Yet hastow caught a fals suspecioun.
I will hym noght, thogh thou wert deed tomorwe."'

Compare lines 293-302 with Theophrastus, "We must always be looking at her face, and we must always praise her beauty: if we look at another woman, she thinks that she is not loved anymore. She must be called, 'My lady,' her birthday must be celebrated; we must swear oaths to her health and wish her long life. We have to show respect to her nurse, her old nursemaid, her father's servant, her foster-child, her handsome follower … Upon whomsoever she sets her heart, they must have her love though they want her not" (From *The Golden Book of Marriage* Author's version).

'"You say also that it displeases me
Unless you are forever praising my beauty,
And every moment gazing intently on my face,   295
And call me 'fair lady' in every place,
And provide a feast upon my birthday,
And make sure I have new and splendid clothes to wear,
And do my old nurse every honor,
And likewise my personal maid in my private chamber,   300
And my father's family and his kin."
That is how you talk, you old barrel-full of lies!
      '"And just because our apprentice, Jankin,
With his crisp hair, shining as fine as gold,
Chivalrously attends me everywhere I go,   305
You become suspicious without any justification.
      I would not want him even if you died tomorrow!"'

The dutiful wife as medieval homemaker.
(Source unknown. Public domain)

"'But tel me this, why hydestow, with sorwe,
The keyes of thy cheste awey fro me?
It is my good as wel as thyne, pardee! 310
What, wenestow make an idiot of oure dame?
Now, by that lord that called is Seint Jame,
Thou shalt nat bothe, thogh that thou wert wood,
Be maister of my body and my good;
The oon thou shalt forgo, maugree thyne yen. 315
What nedeth thee of me to enquere and spyen?
I trow thou woldest loke me in thy chiste!
    "'Thou sholdest seye, 'Fair wyfe, go wher thee liste;
Taak youre disport; I wol nat leve no talis;
I knowe yow for a trewe wyf, Dame Alis." 320
    "'We love no man that taketh kepe or charge
Wher that we goon; we wol ben at oure large.'"

In describing to her husband's suspicions of her relationship with their apprentice Jankin, the Wife is referring specifically to her fourth husband. Ironically, one has only to read her glowing description of Jankin's hair to know how totally justified was her husband's jealousy!

In lines 313-5, we see the first version of the choice which the knight will be given at the end of Alison's tale: here, the husband may have his wife's money (upon their marriage everything owned by the wife had become legally the husband's property) or her body (that is, have her love, as expressed in willing sexual intercourse). Not only is the question stated clearly, but Alison provides the answer: the husband should give up trying to control the wife and should trust her to be mistress of her own reputation. No indication is yet given of the complete change which this would make (for the better) in their relationship.

58

"'But tell me this, why do you hide (may it bring you sorrow),
The keys of your chest away from me?
It is my property as well as yours, that I know!   310
What, do you thing that you will make an idiot of your mistress?
Now, by that lord who is called Saint James [of Compostella],
Even if you get mad at me, you shall not both
Be master of my body and of my goods.
One you shall give up, for all your spying.   315
What need have you to enquire about or spy on me?
I think you would like to lock me in your chest!
    "'You should say: 'Wife, go where you wish.
Take your pleasure; I will not listen to gossip.
I know you for a true wife, Dame Alice."   320
    "'We love no man that keeps watch and sets limits on

Where we go; we wish to have our freedom.'"

A medieval wedding.(Source unknown. Public domain.)

"'Of alle men, yblessed moot he be,
The wyse astrologien Daun Ptholeme,
That seith this proverbe in his *Almageste*:   325
'Of alle men, his wisdom is the hyeste
That rekketh nevere who hath the world in honde.'
By this proverbe thou shalt well understonde,
Have thou ynogh, what thar thee recche or care
How mirily that othere folkes fare?   330
For, certeyn, olde dotard, by youre leve,
Ye shul have queynte right ynogh at eve.
He is to greet a nigard that wolde werne
A man to lighte his candle at his lanterne;
He shal have never the lasse light, pardee.   335
Have thou ynogh, thee thar not pleyne thee.
    "'Thou syest also, if that we make us gay
With clothing and with precious array,
That it is peril of oure chastitee.
And yet, with sorrow, thou enforcest thee,   340
And seye thise wordes in th'Apostles name,
'In habit made with chastitee and shame
Ye wommen shul apparaille yow,' quod he,
'And noght in tressed heer and gay perree,
As perles, ne gold, ne clothes riche.'   345
After thy text, ne after thy rubriche,
I will not wirche as muchel as a gnat.'"

The use of the word "queynte" (332) is not a double entendre. There is nothing subtle about this direct naming of a woman's sexual organ; Alison intends it to be direct and shocking, though probably not so offensive as the modern reader might find such a reference. This reminds us of Chaucer's apology in *The General Prologue*, "But first, I pray you, of your courtesy, / That you will not ascribe it to my lack of culture, / Even though I speak plainly of this narrative, / Presenting to you their words and behavior; / Even if I use their exact words. / For this you know as well as I do: / Whoever repeats a tale told by another man, / He must report, as nearly as he is able, / Every single word, if he can, / Even if that means that he speaks very rudely and directly, / Or else he must tell his tale inaccurately, / Or make something up, or substitute different words" (Author's modernization 727-738). As someone who is not at all offended by talk about sexual organs and sexual relationships, one can sense the Wife's delight in shocking her hearers.

"'Of all men, the most blessed must be,
That wise astrologer, Master Ptolemy,
Who wrote this proverb in his *Almagest*:   325
'Of all men his wisdom is the highest
Who cares not who controls the world.'
By this proverb you must clearly understand,
That if you have enough, why should you worry
How well other folks are getting along?   330
Be sure, old dotard, by your leave
You shall have all the sexual pleasure you wish at night.
He is too great a miser who will refuse
A man who wants to take a light from his lantern;
He will have no less light by doing that, I know!   335
If you have enough, there is no need to complain.
        "'You say too, if we make ourselves attractive
With clothing, and finery,
It puts our virtue in peril.
And yet (curse you) you support your point   340
With these words of the Apostle Paul,
'In modest clothing
You women shall dress yourselves,' said he,
'And not with braided hair, or brilliant jewelry,
Such as pearls, nor with gold, nor with expensive clothes.' 345
I will not act in accord with your text,
As much as a gnat would!'"

The Wife's husband cites St. Paul who writes in 1 Timothy ii 9-10: "In like manner also, that women adorn themselves in modest apparel, with shamefacedness and sobriety; not with broided hair, or gold, or pearls, or costly array; But (which becometh women professing godliness) with good works" (King James). Her rejection of his "rubriche" (literally meaning the portion of the text highlighted in red) may well be influenced by her knowledge of what comes immediately after it: "Let the woman learn in silence with all subjection. But I suffer not a woman to teach, nor to usurp authority over the man, but to be in silence" (1 Timothy ii 11-12, King James).

'"Thou seydest this, that I was lyk a cat;
For whoso wolde senge a cattes skyn,
Thanne wolde the cat wel dwellen in his in;   350
And if the cattes skyn be slyk and gay,
She wol nat dwelle in house half a day,
But forth she wole, er any day be dawed,
To shewe hir skyn, and goon a-caterwawed.
This is to seye, if I be gay, sire shrewe,   355
I wol renne out, my borel for to shewe.
    '"Sire olde fool, what eyleth [helpeth] thee to spyen?
Thogh thou preye Argus with hise hundred eyen
To be my wardeecors, as he kan best,
In feith, he shal nat kepe me but me lest -   360
Yet koude I make his berd, so moot I thee!
    '"Thou seydest eek that ther been thynges thre,
The whiche thynges troublen al this erthe,
And that no wight ne may endure the ferthe.
O leeve sire shrewe, Jhesu shorte thy lyf!   365
Yet prechestow and seyst an hateful wyf
Yrekened is for oon of thise meschances.
Been ther none othere maner resemblances
That ye may lykne youre parables to,
But if a sely wyf be oon of tho?   370
    '"Thou lyknest, eek, wommenes love to helle,
To bareyne lond, ther water may nat dwelle.
Thou lyknest it also to wylde fyr:
The moore it brenneth, the moore it hath desyr
To consume every thyng that brent wole be.   375
Thou seyest, right as wormes shende a tree,
Right so a wyf destroyeth hire housbonde;
This knowe they that been to wyves bonde."'

In Greek mythology, Argus Panoptes was an all-seeing giant with one
hundred eyes only a few of which would be closed in sleep at any one time.
    The husbands' supposed references to things which trouble the earth is
from Proverbs xxx 21-3:"For three things the earth is perturbed, Yes, for four
it cannot bear up: For a servant when he reigns, A fool when he is filled with
food, A hateful woman when she is married, And a maidservant who
succeeds her mistress."

"'You also said that I was like a cat in going out,
For whosoever would singe a cat's fur
Then will the cat stay inside the house;   350
But if the cat's fur be smooth and sleek,
She will not dwell in that house half a day.
But out she will pad everyday before dawn,
To show her fine fur, and go looking for a mate.
What you mean is to say that if I look attractive, Sir Trouble,   355
I'll run and show off my humble clothes to everyone.
    "'Sir Old Fool, what use to you are spies?
Though you beg Argus with his hundred eyes
To be my bodyguard, since he best knows how,
In faith, he shall not restrain me if it is not my wish.   360
I could outwit him, I assure you!
    "'Then you said that there are three things,
Which trouble all this earth,
And that no man can endure the fourth.
Be quiet, Sir Trouble, may Jesus shorten your life!   365
Still you preach and say that a hateful wife
Is included as one of these calamities.
Are there then no other comparisons
You could address your parables to,
Without an innocent wife becoming a target for them?   370
    "'You even liken woman's love to Hell,
To barren land, where water is absent.
You liken it then, as well, to a wild fire:
The more it burns, the more it strengthens
To consume everything that can be burnt.   375
You say that just as insects kill a tree,
Just so a wife destroys her husband;
And that those who are chained to a wife know this.'"

'Lordynges, right thus, as ye have understonde,
Baar I stifly myne olde housbondes on honde   380
That thus they seyden in hir dronkenesse;
And al was fals, but that I took witnesse
On Janekyn, and on my nece also.
O Lord! The peyne I dide hem and the wo,
Ful giltelees, by Goddes sweete pyne!   385
For as an hors I koude byte and whyne;
I koude pleyne, and yit was in the gilt,
Or elles often tyme hadde I been spilt -
Whose that first to mille comth, first grint;
I pleyned first, so was oure werre ystint.   390
They were ful glade to excuse hem blyve
Of thyng of which they nevere agilte hir lyve!
      'Of wenches wolde I beren hem on honde,
Whan that for syk unnethes myghte he stonde.
Yet tikled I his herte, for that he   395
Wende that I hadde of him so greet chiertee!
I swoor that al my walkinge out by nighte
Was for t'espye wenches that he dighte;
Under that colour hadde I many a mirthe.
For al swich wit is yeven us in oure birthe: 400
Deceite, weping, spynning, God hath yive
To wommen kyndely, whil that they may live.'

The reader will notice that the Wife switches between plural pronouns
("they ... hem ... hir") and singular pronouns ("he ... him ... his"), but in my
modernization I have stuck with the plural. Alison appears to be talking of
her first three husbands, but the reference to Jankin can only refer to husband
number four. However, there is no doubt that what she says of one applies to
all of her first four husbands: each was older than the Wife and each she
dominated totally. The only difference was that the fourth husband was not
an old man and that he vigorously asserted mastery in the marriage and
opposed her will, though ineffectively since he was no match for her
determination and cunning.

'Masters, just in this way, as you have understood,
Did I firmly keep my old husbands in hand   380
Claiming that they had said these things when they were drunk;
And it was all lies, but yet I made witnesses
Of Jankin, and of my niece also, to support my accusations.
O Lord! The pain and sorrow I gave them,
Yet they were guiltless, by God's sweet suffering!   385
For I could like a horse can both bite and whinny.
I could complain, though I was the guilty one,
Or else, full many a time, I would have been ruined.
Whoso comes first to the mill first gets to grind his grain;
I whimpered first and so I won our battles.   390
They were very happy quickly to excuse
Things they had never done in their lives!
      'With wenching would I accuse them, by this hand,
When for illness they could hardly stand.
Yet I delighted the hearts of them so much that they   395
Deemed it was love and affection that produced such jealousy!
I swore that all my walking out at night
Was but to spy on girls they were sleeping with;
And under cover of that I had a lot of fun.
For all such cunning is given to us at our birth: 400
Deceit, weeping, and spinning tales, God gives
To women by nature for the course of their lives.'

'And thus of o thing I avaunte me:
Atte ende I hadde the bettre in ech degree,
By sleighte, or force, or by som maner thing,   405
As by continuel murmur or grucching.
Namely abedde hadden they meschaunce:
Ther wolde I chyde, and do hem no plesaunce.
I wolde no lenger in the bed abyde,
If that I felte his arm over my syde,   410
Til he had maad his raunson unto me -
Thanne wolde I suffre hym do his nycetee.
    'And therfore every man this tale I telle,
Winne whose may, for al is for to selle:
With empty hand men may none haukes lure.   415
For winning wolde I al his lust endure,
And make me feyned appetyt
(And yet in bacon hadde I nevere delyt)
That made me that evere I wolde hem chyde.
For thogh the Pope hadde seten hem bisyde,   420
I wolde nat spare hem at hir owene bord,
For, by my trouthe, I quitte hem word for word.
As helpe me verray God omnipotent,
Thogh I right now sholde make my testament,
I ne owe hem nat a word that it nys quit.   425
I broghte it so aboute, by my wit,
That they moste yeve it up, as for the beste,
Or elles hadde we nevere been in reste.
For thogh he looked as a wood leoun,
Yet sholde he faille of his conclusioun.'   430

There is an evident contradiction in the account which the Wife gives here of her sexual relations with her husbands and what she said earlier (see lines 196-216). Previously, she characterized her first three husbands as too old for sex and boasted about making them work all night to satisfy her, but here it is the men who want sex and Alison who uses their lust (she claims to have none herself) to bully them into giving her financial and other concessions. Probably Alison simply used whichever tactic seemed most likely to succeed at the time.

Alison's assertion that, before she would allow her husbands to have sex with her, she ensured that "he had maad his raunson" (411) is ambiguous, but her later assertion that "For winning wolde I al his lust endure" (416) makes

'And thus I may boast of one thing:
In the end, I got the better of them every step of the way,
By trick, or coercion, or by some other strategy,   405
Such as by continual grumbling and grousing.
Especially in bed they had a hard time:
There would I berate them and give them no pleasure.
I would not even stay in the bed
When I felt his arm come over my side,   410
Till he had paid his fine unto me -
Then would I let him do his little thing.
    'And therefore I tell this tale to all men,
Profit by it whoever may, for I offer it all for sale:
With an empty hand, men can never lure falcons.   415
For my own profit I would put up with all his lust,
And pretend to have a sexual appetite for him
(Even though I have never liked bacon)
And that is why I used to nag them so much.
Even if the Pope were seated beside them   420
I would not have spared them at their own table,
For, on my honor, I repaid them word for word.
So help me the True God Omnipotent,
Though I should make my last will and testament right now,
I owe them not a single word that was not paid back in full.   425
I so contrived things, and by my cunning,
That they must give it up, as for the best,
Or otherwise we would never have had any quiet.
For though he glared like a raging lion,
Yet I made sure he would fail to gain his objective in the end.'   430

it clear that her husbands had to pay her to have sex, that is, that they had to give up their attempt to secure all of the couple's material possessions in their own hands as the law gave them every right to do. The Wife compares having sex with her old husbands with eating bacon - both are equally distasteful. Dried, smoked, and salted bacon was the staple meat of the poorer classes particularly in winter. They probably got pretty sick of it!

Economic references proliferate ("'maad his raunson … to selle … For winning … I ne owe hem'"). Wetherbee explains Alison's inability to escape commercial metaphor when discussing her relationships with her husbands, "Placed on the marriage market at the age of twelve, she finds it difficult to value herself in any but economic terms" (78).

'Thanne wolde I seye, "Goode lief, taak keepe
How mekely loketh Wilkyn, oure sheepe.
Com neer, my spouse, lat me ba thy cheke.
Ye sholde been al pacient and meke,
And han a swete spyced conscience,   435
Sith ye so preche of Jobes pacience.
Suffreth alwey, sin ye so wel kan preche,
And but ye do, certeyn we shal yow teche
That it is fair to have a wyf in pees.
Oon of us two moste bowen, doutelees,   440
And sith a man is more resonable
Than womman is, ye moste been suffrable.
What eyleth yow to grucche thus and grone?
Is it for ye wolde have my queynte allone?
Wy, taak it al! Lo, have it every deel!   445
Peter, I shrewe yow, but ye love it weel!
For if I wolde selle my *bele chose*,
I koude walke as fressh as is a rose;
But I wol kepe it for youre owene tooth.
Ye be to blame, by God! I sey yow sooth!"   450
Swiche manere wordes hadde we on honde.
Now wol I speken of my fourthe housbonde.'

In describing her sexual organ, the Wife uses "bele chose" [pretty thing] (447) as a euphemism - the French sounds rather courtly and impressive. This is, of course, in sharp contrast to her use of the word "queynte" (444) which is calling a spade a spade!

Apparently the husbands were oblivious to Alison's mockery of them when she recommended that they adopt the same attitude as their sheep - an animal not noted for its intelligence. Notice how she continues the joke by offering to "ba" them on the cheek, mockingly repeating the sound a sheep makes (as in the later nursery rhyme *Baa Baa Black Sheep*), and still the husbands do not see that they are being mocked!

The Wife says that she is now going to speak about her fourth husband, but the earlier reference to a husband's jealousy of her relationship with Jankin can only refer to the fourth husband. The reader assumes that nearly everything she has just said about her methods of getting the upper hand applies to all four husbands, and that she is now going to talk about what made her fourth different from her three 'good' husbands.

68

'Then I would say, "Sweetheart, consider
How docile is our sheep, Wilkin.
Come near, my spouse, let me kiss your cheek!
You should be always patient and docile,
And have a sweetly seasoned disposition,   435
Since you preach so much about Job's patience.
Endure suffering at all times, since that's what you preach so well;
And unless you do, be sure that we women will teach
That it is a good thing to leave a wife in peace.
Undoubtedly, one of us two must submit to the other,   440
And since a man is by nature more rational,
Than a woman is, you must have tolerance.
What ails you that you grumble thus and grouse?
Is it because you would have my sex all to yourself?
Why take it all! Have every bit of it!   445
By Saint Peter, curse you, but you are very fond of it!
Now, if I chose to go sell my pretty thing,
I could afford to walk out looking as radiant as a rose,
But I will keep it for your own lusty appetite.
You are to blame, by God! I tell the truth."   450
Such were the kinds of words we had between us constantly.
Now will I tell you of my fourth husband.'

'My fourthe housbonde was a revelour,
This is to seyn, he hadde a paramour,
And I was yong and ful of ragerye,   455
Stiborne and strong, and joly as a pye.
How koude I daunce to an harpe smale,
And synge, ywis, as any nyghtyngale
Whan I had dronke a draughte of swete wyn!
Metellius, the foule cherl, the swyn,   460
That with a staf birafte his wyf hir lyf,
For she drank wyn, thogh I hadde been his wyf
He sholde nat han daunted me fro drinke!
And after wyn, on Venus moste I thinke,
For al so siker as cold engendreth hayl,   465
A likerous mouth moste han a likerous tayl.
In wommen vinolent is no defence -
This knowen lecchours by experience.
    'But, Lord Crist! whan that it remembreth me
Upon my yowthe, and on my jolitee,   470
It tikleth me aboute myn herte roote.
Unto this day it dooth myn herte boote
That I have had my world as in my tyme.
But age, allas! that al wole envenyme,
Hath me biraft my beautee and my pith.   475
Lat go, farewel, the devel go therwith!
The flour is goon; ther is namoore to telle:
The bren, as I best kan, now moste I selle.
But yet to be right myrie wol I fonde.
Now wol I tellen of my fourthe housbonde.'   480

    The reference to the Wife's love of dancing and singing to "an harpe
smale" (457), that is a small harp held on the lap (as opposed to a large harp
which would rest on the floor) seems to me to be another euphemism for
sexual activity. If there is any doubt about that identification, there can be
none at all in the Wife's reference to "a likerous tayl" (466) since the word
'tail' still retains a sexual connotation in modern colloquial usage.
    Once again, the Wife goes off at a tangent: she manages only two lines
about her fourth husband before she turns to describing her own youthful
vitality at the time she married him. There is genuine pathos in the Wife's
description of her now faded beauty and diminished vigor; this lady is deeply

'My fourth husband, he was a reveler,
That is to say, he kept a mistress,
And I young and full of passion,   455
Stubborn and strong-willed, and merry as a magpie.
How I could dance to the tune of a small harp,
And sing, truly, as sweetly as any nightingale
When I had drunk a draught of sweet wine!
Metellius, the foul churl, the swine,   460
Who beat his wife to death with a staff
Because she drank wine - if I had been his wife
He never should have frightened me from drink!
And after wine, my thoughts must turn to sex,
For just as surely as cold produces hail,   465
A mouth thirsty for self-indulgence implies a similar tail.
Wine leaves women defenseless -
This all seducers know by experience.
    'But Lord Christ! When I reflect
Upon my youth and on my love of life,   470
It tickles the bottom of my heart.
To this day, it makes my heart feel glad
That I have lived my life to the full.
But age, alas, that poisons everything,
Has taken away my looks and my vigor;   475
Let it go, farewell, the devil go with it!
The flour is gone; there is no more to tell:
As best I can, I must I now sell the bran.
But yet I will strive to be thoroughly happy.
Now will I tell you of my fourth husband.'   480

aware of her own fading looks and of her mortality. Nevertheless, the reader
cannot but admire her determination to live her life to the full while she can.

    Compare lines 469-75 with the following from Jean de Meun, "I was a
very great beauty, but now I must complain and moan that my face has lost
its charms ... Oh God! The memories give me pleasure, and when I think
back to the gay life that my heart so yearns, my thoughts are filled with
delight and my limbs with new vigor. The thought and the recollection of it
make my whole body young again" (From *The Romance of the Rose*
Author's version).

'I seye, I hadde in herte greet despyt
That he of any oother had delyt,
But he was quit, by God and by Seint Joce!
I made hym of the same wode a croce,
Nat of my body, in no foul manere,   485
But certeynly, I made folk swich cheere
That in his owene grece I made hym frye
For angre, and for verray jalousye.
By God! In erthe I was his purgatorie,
For which I hope his soule be in glorie.   490
For, God it woot, he sat ful ofte and song,
Whan that his shoo ful bitterly him wrong.
Ther was no wight, save God and he, that wiste,
In many wyse how soore I him twiste.
    'He deyde whan I cam fro Jerusalem,   495
And lyth ygrave under the roode beem.
Al is his tombe noght so curius
As was the sepulcre of him Darius,
Which that Appeles wroghte subtilly -
It nys but wast to burye him preciously.   500
Lat hym fare wel, God yeve his soul reste!
He is now in his grave and in his cheste.'

Getting the better of her fourth husband was a question of turning the tables on him: since he made Alison jealous by his infidelity, she made a cross of the same wood. However, the Wife is careful to make it clear that her revenge was "Nat of my body, in no foul manere" (485), by which she means that she did not actually have sex with another man, rather she created the suspicion in her husband's mind that she was having altogether too much fun in her social life. The husband's imagination did the rest!

Alison's justification of the economy with which she buried husband number four is comic - it would just have been a waste of money since he was dead! It is entirely consistent that a woman who thought throughout her first three marriages of increasing her wealth should save money on a tomb.

St. Judocus is a rather obscure Breton saint. The son of Prince Juthael, King of Brittany, he renounced his title and wealth and lived out his life as a hermit. Presumably Alison includes his name in her oath because she certainly was not going to give up either her freedom or her goods.

'I say that in my heart I was outraged
When he took his pleasure with any other woman.
But he was paid back, by God and by Saint Joce!
I made for him a cross of the same wood,
Not with my body and any unclean manner,   485
But certainly I made people so merry
That in his own fat I made him fry
In anger and utter jealousy.
By God, on earth I was his purgatory,
For which I hope his soul lives now in glory!   490
For God knows, many a time he sat down and sang out
When the shoe bitterly pinched his foot.
There was no one, except God and himself, that knew
In how many ways I would torment him.
    'He died while I was returning from Jerusalem,   495
And lies entombed beneath the great rood-beam [that separates the
nave from the chancel in our church].
Although his tomb is not so elaborately adorned
As was the sepulcher of Darius,
The one which Apelles made so skillfully -
It would only have been a waste to bury him expensively.   500
Fare him well. God give his soul good rest,
He now is in the grave and in his coffin.'

A medieval doctor administers an herbal remedy. Such potions were, of course, no remedy for serious illnesses such as the plague.
(Medieval manuscript. Source unknown. Public domain.)

'Now of my fifthe housbonde wol I telle -
God lete his soule nevere come in helle!
And yet was he to me the mooste shrewe;   505
That feele I on my ribbes al by rewe,
And evere shal unto myn ending day.
But in oure bed he was so fressh and gay,
And therwithal so wel koude he me glose,
Whan that he wolde han my *bele chose*,   510
That thogh he hadde me bete on every boon,
He koude winne agayn my love anoon.
I trowe I loved him beste for that he
Was of his love daungerous to me!
We wommen han, if that I shal nat lye,   515
In this matere a queynte fantasye;
Wayte what thing we may nat lightly have,
Therafter wol we crye al day and crave.
Forbede us thing, and that desyren we;
Preesse on us faste, and thanne wol we flee.   520
With daunger oute we al oure chaffare;
Greet prees at market maketh deere ware,
And to greet cheep is holde at litel prys.
This knoweth every womman that is wys.
'My fifthe housbonde, God his soule blesse!   525
Which that I took for love, and no richesse,
He som tyme was a clerk of Oxenford,
And hadde left scole, and wente at hoom to bord
With my gossib, dwellinge in oure toun -
God have hir soule! Hir name was Alisoun.   530
She knew myn herte, and eek my pryvetee,
Bet than oure parisshe preest, so moot I thee!'

The tone in which Alison speaks of her last husband is very different from the way in which she has talked of numbers one to four. Jankin was like her fourth husband in that he claimed sovereignty in marriage, but unlike him in that the Wife loved him. Notice that, as soon as she speaks of him, she calls on God to bless his departed soul (504 and 525).

The Wife continues to spice up her account with euphemisms. The adjective in "a queynte fantasye" (516) means only a peculiar or perverse trait, but we have already established the sexual meaning of the same word as

'And now of my fifth husband will I tell -
God grant his soul may never go to Hell!
And yet he was to me the cruelest rascal;   505
I can still feel it on my ribs every one,
And ever shall, until my dying day.
But in our bed he was so energetic and joyful,
And additionally he could so coax and flatter me,
Whenever he wanted to have my pretty thing,   510
That though he had beaten me on every bone,
He could win back my love immediately.
I believe I loved him best of all because he
Gave of his love most grudgingly to me.
We women have, if I am not to lie,   515
In this matter of love, a strange perversity;
Take note that the thing we cannot easily have,
And for that we will cry and crave all day long.
Forbid us something, and that thing will we covet;
Insist upon it, then will we turn and run.   520
Reluctantly, we set out our goods;
Great crowds at market force up the prices,
And what is too cheap is little sought after.
All this knows every woman who is wise.
        'My fifth husband, may God bless his spirit!   525
Whom I took only for love, and not for his wealth,
Had been sometime a student at Oxford University,
And had left school and came as a boarder in the house
Of my best friend, living in our town -
God save her soul! Her name was Alison.   530
'She knew my deepest feelings and all my most private thoughts
Better than did our parish priest, I promise you!'

a noun. It seems clear that, for the first time in her life, Alison found sexual
fulfillment with Jankin.

'To hire biwreyed I my conseil al,
For hadde myn housbonde pissed on a wal,
Or doon a thing that sholde han cost his lyf,   535
To hire, and to another worthy wyf,
And to my nece, which that I loved weel,
I wolde han toold his conseil every deel.
And so I dide ful often, God it woot,
That made his face often reed and hoot   540
For verray shame, and blamed himself for he
Had toold to me so greet a pryvetee.
      'And so bifel that ones in a Lente
So often tymes I to my gossyb wente
(For evere yet I lovede to be gay,   545
And for to walke in March, Averille, and May,
Fro hous to hous, to heere sondry talis),
That Jankyn clerk, and my gossyb Dame Alis,
And I myself, into the feeldes wente.
Myn housbonde was at Londoun al that Lente;   550
I hadde the bettre leyser for to pleye,
And for to see, and eek for to be seye
Of lusty folk. What wiste I wher my grace
Was shapen for to be, or in what place?
Therfore I made my visitaciouns   555
To vigilies and to processiouns,
To preching, eek, and to thise pilgrimages,
To pleyes of miracles, and to mariages,
And wered upon my gaye scarlet gytes.'

   Lent is the forty days after Easter which are set aside for fasting, prayer, and penance. People traditionally give up some luxury or something that they really like at this time. For the Wife, however, Lent means the coming of spring and the opportunity, after a long, cold, wet winter, to get out and about. The enthusiasm for the rebirth of nature in lines 546-559 reflects the opening of *The General Prologue* itself, "When the sweet showers of April / Have penetrated to the roots after the dry month of March / And bathed in moisture every vein of the plants / Which causes the flowers to come into blossom; / When, also, the West Wind, with his fragrant breath, has / In every wood and field breathed life / Into the tender shoots and buds, and the young sun / Has run half his course into the sign of Aries the Ram, / And small birds sing melodiously / That sleep all through the night with their eyes

76

'To her I confided all my secrets.
For if my husband had pissed against a wall,
Or done something that might have cost his life,   535
To her, and to another worthy woman,
And to my niece, who I always loved deeply,
I would have told his secret in every detail,
And I did so, many, many times, God knows,
Which often made his face deep red and hot with blushing   540
For utter shame, and he blamed himself because he
Had told me such a personal secret.
    'So it befell that once in Lent
I went very often to my dear friend
(For even then I loved always to enjoy myself   545
And to walk out in March, April, and May,
From house to house, to hear the latest gossip),
That Jankin, the clerk, and my friend Dame Alis,
And I myself walked out into the meadows.
My husband was in London all that Lent,   550
So I had the greater freedom, then, to socialize,
To observe others, and to be seen myself
By lively folk. What did I care where my luck
Was destined to find me, or in what place?
Therefore, I made my visits round about   555
To vigils and religious processions,
To preaching too, and shrines of pilgrimage,
To miracle plays, and to marriages,
And wore my bright scarlet gowns.'

/ (Because Nature so urges them in their amorous desires); / Then folk long to go on pilgrimages…" (1-12 Author's modernization).

The old woman in *The Romance of the Rose* counsels that "A woman must be careful not to shut herself away, for the more she stays at home, the less she is seen by everyone and the less her beauty is known, desired, and sought after. She ought often to go to the principal church and attend weddings, processions, games, festivals, and dances, for in such places that the God and Goddess of Love hold their schools and sing Mass to their disciples" (Author's version).

'Thise wormes, ne thise motthes, ne thise mytes,   560
Upon my peril, frete hem never a deel;
And wostow why? For they were used weel!
    'Now wol I tellen forth what happed me.
I seye that in the feeldes walked we,
Til trewely we hadde swich daliance,   565
This clerk and I, that of my purveyance
I spak to hym, and seyde hym how that he,
If I were wydwe, sholde wedde me.
For certeynly, I sey for no bobance,
Yet was I nevere withouten purveyance   570
Of mariage, n'of othere thinges eek.
I holde a mouses herte nat worth a leek
That hath but oon hole for to sterte to,
And if that faille, thanne is al ydo.
    'I bar him on honde he hadde enchanted me   575
(My dame taughte me that soutiltee.),
And eek I seyde I mette of him al night,
He wolde han slayn me as I lay upright,
And al my bed was ful of verray blood,
But yet I hope that he shal do me good,   580
For blood bitokeneth gold, as me was taught.
And al was fals; I dremed of it right naught,
But as I folwed ay my dames loore,
As wel of this as of othere thinges moore.
    'But now, sire, lat me se, what I shal seyn?   585
Aha! By God, I have my tale ageyn!'

Having promised to describe her fifth husband, the Wife has got carried
away with an account of her own feelings during the Lent when, in the
absence of her fourth husband, she used her feminine wiles to seduce Jankin
and to give a self-congratulatory account of her foresight. Not for the first
time, she has to remind herself of what it is that she should be talking about
(585-6).

The dream which she recounts is clearly a sexual fantasy designed to
titillate Jankin: she is lying on her back, defenseless, and he kills her.
'Killing' and 'dying' are common euphemisms for the climax of the sexual
act, and the description of blood suggests the deflowering of a virgin.

Alison's reference to her hope that Jankin would bring her wealth is
ironic given their relative social positions, but it is cunningly designed to

'Neither these grubs, nor these moths, nor these mites,   560
I say it upon my life, ever got so much as a bite out of my clothes;
And do know you why? Because I wore them constantly!
    'Now will I tell you what happened to me.
I say that in the meadows we walked
Till, truly, we had such flirtation chatter,   565
This clerk and I, that about my plans for the future,
I spoke to him, and told him how he,
If I were a widow, should marry me.
For certainly, I say it not meaning to brag,
But I was never without foresight   570
With regard to marriage, nor in other matters.
I hold a mouse's heart not worth a leek
Who has only one bolt-hole into which to run,
And if that fails, then it is all over.
    'I convinced him that he had enchanted me   575
(My mother taught me all that ploy.),
And then I said I had dreamed of him all night,
That he would have slain me as I lay face upward on my back,
And all my bed was saturated with blood,
But still, I hoped that this meant he would bring me good fortune,
Because blood symbolizes gold, as I was taught.   581
And all was false, I dreamed of him not at all,
I was just following my mother's teaching,
As well in this as in many other things.
    'But now, let's see, what was I going to say?   585
Oh yes! By God, I have the thread of my story again!'

suggest to Jankin the financial advantages of marrying his master's widow despite the twenty-year disparity in their ages.

Although the Wife's reference to following the advice of her "dame" (576 and 583) is normally seen as a reference to her mother, Cigman makes a good case that she is actually referring to the natural cunning which she gets from Venus, her ruling planet (155-6).

Compare lines 569-74 with Jean de Meun, "The mouse who has only one hole for retreat has a very poor refuge and is in great danger when he goes foraging. It is just the same for a woman … it [is] a very foolish idea to have only one lover" (From the *Romance of the Rose* Author's version).

'Whan that my fourthe housbonde was on beere,
I weep algate, and made sory cheere
(As wyves mooten, for it is usage),
And with my coverchief covered my visage,   590
But for that I was purveyed of a make,
I wepte but smale, and that I undertake.
    'To chirche was myn housbonde born a-morwe
With neighebores, that for him maden sorwe,
And Jankyn, oure clerk, was oon of tho.   595
As help me God! Whan that I saugh him go
After the beere, me thoughte he hadde a paire
Of legges and of feet so clene and faire
That al myn herte I yaf unto his hoold.
He was, I trowe, a twenty winter oold,   600
And I was fourty, if I shal seye sooth;
But yet I hadde alwey a coltes tooth.
Gat-tothed I was, and that bicam me weel;
I hadde the prente of Seinte Venus seel.
As help me God! I was a lusty oon,   605
And faire, and riche, and yong, and wel-bigoon;
And trewely, as myne housbondes tolde me,
I hadde the beste quoniam mighte be.
    'For certes, I am al Venerien
In feelinge, and myn herte is Marcien:
Venus me yaf my lust, my likerousnesse,   610
And Mars yaf me my sturdy hardinesse.
Myn ascendent was Taur, and Mars therinne.
Allas! Allas! That evere love was synne!'

One cannot help but admire the honesty of the Wife's admission (or
boast) that she so admired the shape of Jankin's legs as he walked behind her
husband's coffin that she completely gave him her heart. She has no
conscience at all about having faked the tears for her dead husband.

Alison is perfectly content with the person she is. She accepts that her
nature has been determined by her birth signs and has no desire to control, or
to feel guilty about, the impulses thus created. She is aware, however, that
her outlook on life and love puts her at odds with a male-dominated society
which sees women as inferior creatures and physical love as contrary to
spiritual growth, and that this has caused her much conflict and some
unhappiness during her life.

'When my fourth husband lay upon his bier,
I wept appropriately and made a great show of grief
(As wives must, for it is expected of them),
And with my headscarf covered up my face.   590
But since I was already provided with a mate,
I really wept but little, I can assure you.
    'To church my husband was carried next morning
By neighbors, who grieved for him,
And Jankin, our clerk, was among them.   595
So help me God! When I saw him walking
After the bier, I thought he had a fine pair
Of legs and feet so well-formed and so beautiful
That I completely gave him all my heart.
He was, I think, only twenty winters old,   600
And I was forty, if I tell the truth;
But then I had not lost my youthful appetites.
Gap-toothed I was, and that suited me well;
I had the birthmark of Saint Venus' seal.
So help me God! I was a lively one,   605
And beautiful, and rich, and young, and well provided for;
And truly, as my husbands all assured me,
I had the most perfect pudendum imaginable.
    'For truly, my nature is entirely controlled by Venus
In feeling, and my brain is controlled by Mars:
Venus gave me my vigor, my sexual appetite,   610
And Mars gave me my bold assertiveness.
At my birth, Taurus was my ascendant sign, with Mars therein.
Alas! Alas! That ever love was sin!'

    A gap between the front teeth, especially in women, has traditionally
been associated with lustful characteristics. Chaucer would have known this
both from folk traditions and from medieval books of physiognomy.
Obviously there is no scientific basis for this association. Men in mny
cultures seem to find the feature attractive, and so it is ambiguously
associated both with beauty and with loose morals. Alison explicitly
identifies the gap between her front teeth as the mark of Venus, though I
have been unable to find a convincing reason for the connection of the two.

'I folwed ay myn inclinacioun   615
By vertu of my constellacioun;
That made me I koude noght withdrawe
My chambre of Venus from a good felawe.
Yet have I Martes mark upon my face,
And also in another privee place.   620
For God so wys be my savacioun,
I ne loved nevere by no discrecioun,
But evere folwede myn appetyt
Al were he short, or long, or blak, or whyt.
I took no kep, so that he lyked me,   625
How poore he was, ne eek of what degree.
    'What sholde I seye, but, at the monthes ende,
This joly clerk, Jankyn, that was so hende,
Hath wedded me with greet solempnytee!
And to him yaf I al the lond and fee   630
That evere was me yeven therbifoore.
But afterward repented me ful soore;
He nolde suffre nothing of my list.
By God! He smoot me ones on the list,
For that I rente out of his book a leef,   635
That of the strook myn ere wex al deef.
Stibourn I was as is a leonesse,
And of my tonge verray jangleresse,
And walke I wolde, as I had doon biforn,
From hous to hous, although he had it sworn;   640
For which he often-tymes wolde preche,
And me of olde Romayn geestes teche.'

Astrology holds that the position of the stars and planets at the time of one's birth determines one's character and the future course of one's life. The Wife gets her sociability, generosity and love of pleasure from Venus and her uncompromising aggression from Mars.

What differentiates Jankin from Alison's other husbands is that he has studied at Oxford University and is very well read by the standards of the day. Thus, he is able to use learning, the "auctoritee" (1) of *The Bible*, of classical texts, and of the writings of the Church fathers (like Saint Jerome) to support his misogynist outbursts. Ironically, it is from Jankin that Alison gets most of her own knowledge of textual authority and her ability to use it

'I have always followed my own inclination   615
By virtue of my birth constellation;
Which made me so that I never could withhold
My organ of Venus from a good fellow.
Also, I have the mark of Mars upon my face,
And additionally in another private place.   620
For God so wise be my salvation
For I have never loved prudently,
But have ever followed my own appetite
Whether he was short or tall, or dark or blond.
I took no heed, so long as he cared for me,   625
How poor he was, nor even of what social degree.
   'What should I say now, except that, by the end of the month,
This handsome, lively clerk Jankin,
Had married me with full ceremony,
And to him I gave all of the land and property   630
That had been given me before by my husbands,
Though I later bitterly regretted doing it.
He never allowed me to have my way in anything.
By God, he hit me on the ear, one day,
Because I tore a leaf out of his book,   635
So that as a result my ear has grown totally deaf.
Fierce I was as is a lioness,
And with my tongue a real fighter,
And I would still gad about, as I had done before,
From house to house, though he had sworn that I should not.   640
For which oftentimes he would preach,
And read old Roman tales to teach me.'

in argument.

   Alison, who has been prepared to use marriage to secure material wealth
and to raise her social status is now sufficiently wealthy to marry for love.
Thus, in her fifth marriage, the roles are reversed: Jankin is an attractive
young man, relatively poor, who sees the chance to marry an older woman
who is wealthy. Though we need not see Jankin as a heartless 'gold-digger,'
it is certainly true that he is less motivated to please his wife than is the
infatuated Alison to please him. This is illustrated by the mistake she makes
in transferring all of her property into his hands.

'How he, Symplicius Gallus, lefte his wyf,
And hire forsook, for terme of al his lyf,
Noght but for open-heveded he hir say   645
Lokinge out at his dore upon a day!
        'Another Romayn tolde he me by name,
That, for his wyf was at a someres game
Withouten his witing, he forsook hire eke.
        'And thanne wolde he upon his Bible seke   650
That ilke proverbe of Ecclesiaste
Where he comandeth, and forbedeth faste,
Man shal nat suffre his wyf go roule aboute.
Thanne wolde he seye right thus, withouten doute:
        '"Whoso that buyldeth his hous al of salwes,   655
And priketh his blynde hors over the falwes,
And suffreth his wyf to go seken halwes,
Is worthy to been hanged on the galwes!"
        'But al for noght. I sette noght an hawe
Of his proverbes n'of his olde sawe,   660
Ne I wolde nat of him corrected be.
I hate him that my vyces telleth me,
And so doo mo, God woot, of us than I!
This made hym with me wood al outrely;
I nolde noght forbere him in no cas.   665
        'Now wol I seye yow sooth, by Seint Thomas,
Why that I rente out of his book a leef,
For which he smoot me so that I was deef.'

The classical examples of men who simply dumped their wives for some
perceived misconduct is supported by Ecclesiasticus xxv 26: "If she go not as
thou wouldest have her, cut her off from thy flesh, and give her a bill of
divorce, and let her go" (King James).

Alison's passionate assertion that she hates to be told of her faults finds
an echo in her *Tale*, "ther is noon of us alle, / If any wyght wol clawe us on
the galle, / That we nel kike, for he seith us sooth. / Assay, and he shal fynde
it that so dooth" (939-42).

'How one Sulpicius Gallus left his wife
And forsook her for the rest of his life
For nothing but that he saw her with her head uncovered,   645
Looking out from his doorway one day.
　　'About another Roman he spoke of by name
Who, since his wife was at a summer festival
Without his knowing, he likewise left her.
　　'And then he would search within his Bible   650
For that particular proverb of the old Ecclesiasticus
Where he commands, and firmly forbids,
That a man should allow his wife to gad about;
Then would he repeat this, with total conviction:
　　'"Whoever builds his house out of willow branches,   655
Or spurs his blind horse to run over ploughed fallow fields,
Or lets his wife alone to go visiting shrines on pilgrimage,
Is worthy to be hanged upon the gallows.'"
　　'But it was all for naught; I didn't care a hawthorne berry
For all his proverbs, nor for his old epigrams,   660
Nor yet would I allow myself to be corrected by him.
I hate anyone who tells me my vices,
And so do more of us women (God knows!) than I.
This made him absolutely furious with me,
But I would never yield to him in any circumstance.   665
　　'Now will I tell you the truth, by Saint Thomas à Becket,
About why I tore a leaf from his book,
For which he struck me so it made me deaf.'

'He hadde a book that gladly, night and day,
For his desport, he wolde rede alway;   670
He cleped it *Valerie and Theofraste*,
At which book he lough alwey ful faste.
      'And eek ther was som tyme a clerk at Rome,
A cardinal, that highte Seint Jerome,
That made a book agayn Jovinian.   675
In which book eek ther was Tertulan,
Crisippus, Trotula, and Helowys,
That was abbesse nat fer fro Parys;
And eek the Parables of Salomon,
Ovydes *Art*, and bookes many on,   680
And alle thise were bounden in o volume.
And every nyght and day was his custume,
Whan he hadde leyser and vacacioun
From oother worldly occupacioun,
To reden on this book of wikked wyves.   685
He knew of hem mo legendes and lyves
Than been of goode wyves in the *Bible*.
For trusteth wel, it is an impossible
That any clerk wol speke good of wyves,
But if it be of hooly seintes lyves,   690
Ne of noon oother womman never the mo.'

At the risk of stating the obvious, Jankin reads aloud from his book - no
doubt with appropriate tone and emphasis! Before the age of printing (and, in
fact, well into the nineteenth century) reading at home meant the family
sitting round and hearing someone read aloud, normally in the evening. (Jane
Austen describes her family reading novels, including her own, in this way
with great pleasure.) This book would be a personal anthology, a collection
of manuscript copies custom bound into one large volume.

It is obviously not necessary to know the particular authors and works
contained in Jankin's book in order to get the point: the book was full of
tracts illustrating the folly and perfidy of women. The references are: Walter
Map, *Letter to Valerius*; Theophrastus *On Marriage*; and St. Jerome *Against
Jovian*. Tertullian wrote against remarriage; the name Chrysippus occurs in
St. Jerome; Trotula was a woman doctor who wrote on women's diseases;
and Heloise was forced to give up her love for Abelard and become a nun. In
the cases of Chrysippus and Trotula, Chaucer simply appears to be name-
dropping to impress.

'He had a book that happily, night and day,
For his amusement, he would read continuously.   670
He called it *Valerius and Theophrastus*.
At which book he would always laugh uproarious.
    'And, also, there sometime was a clerk at Rome,
A cardinal called Saint Jerome,
Who wrote a book against Jovinian.   675
In his book, also, there were Tertullian,
Chrysippus, Trotula, and Heloise
Who was the abbess of a nunnery not far from Paris;
And also, the Proverbs of King Solomon,
And Ovid's *Art of Love*, and many other books,   680
And all of these were bound into one volume.
And every night and day, it was his custom,
When he had leisure and took some time off
From all his other business matters,
To read this book about wicked women.   685
He knew of them more stories and more biographies
Than there are good women mentioned in *The Bible*.
For trust me, it is impossible
That any cleric should speak well of women,
Unless it be about the holy lives of saints,   690
But never about any other women.'

A very high-end illuminated medieval
manuscript. (Book of Hours. Paris
about 1410. Wikimedia Commons.
Public domain.)

'Who peyntede the leoun, tel me who?
By God! If wommen hadde writen stories,
As clerkes han withinne hire oratories,
They wolde han writen of men moore wikkednesse   695
Than al the mark of Adam may redresse.
    'The children of Mercurie and of Venus
Been in hir wirking ful contrarious:
Mercurie loveth wisdam and science,
And Venus loveth ryot and dispence.   700
And, for hire dyverse disposicioun,
Ech falleth in otheres exaltacioun.
And thus, God woot, Mercurie is desolat
In Pisces, wher Venus is exaltat;
And Venus falleth ther Mercurie is reysed.   705
Therfore no womman of no clerk is preysed.
The clerk, whan he is old, and may noght do
Of Venus werkes worth his olde sho,
Thanne sit he doun, and writ in his dotage
That wommen kan nat kepe hir marriage.'   710

There are various versions of the fable of the lion (692). One appears in
Aesop and another in Marie de France. All have the same basic point: a man
paints (or sculpts) a man killing a lion, but when the work is shown to the
lion, he points out that there are many occasions when the lion kills the man.
A lion would paint a very different picture because what you see depends on
your point of view.

In reference to line 699, Cigman notes that clerks "who devote their lives
to religion, exemplify the dominance of Mercury" resulting in the
particularly violent conflict between the Wife and Jankin (159-60). Jankin
does not appear to be particularly religious, but as a student at Oxford he
would necessarily have been in minor orders and therefore he represents the
long tradition of clerical misogyny.

'Who painted the lion, answer me that?
By God! If women had written stories,
As have these clerks shut away in their private studies,
They would have written more wickedness of men   695
Than all the men since Adam could put right.
    'Those born under the influence of Mercury and of Venus
Are in their ways of living completely opposite;
For Mercury loves learning and science,
And Venus loves revelry and extravagant spending.   700
And, because of their different dispositions,
The influence of each weakens when the other is in the ascendant.
And God knows Mercury is dejected
In Pisces, wherein Venus is exulted;
And Venus falls when Mercury is raised;   705
That is why no woman is ever praised by a clerk.
A clerk, when he is old and as incapable
Of making love and having fun as is his worn-out shoe,
Then he sits down and writes, in his senility,
That women are incapable of keeping their marriage vows.'   710

A clerk writing against adultery. (Source unknown. Public domain.)

'But now to purpos, why I tolde thee
That I was beten for a book, pardee.
Upon a nyght, Jankyn, that was oure syre,
Redde on his book as he sat by the fyre,
Of Eva first, that for hir wikkednesse   715
Was al mankynde broght to wrecchednesse,
For which that Jhesu Crist himself was slayn,
That boghte us with his herte blood agayn.
Lo, heere expres of womman may ye fynde,
That womman was the los of al mankynde!   720
    'Tho redde he me how Sampson loste his heres;
Slepinge, his lemman kitte it with hir sheres,
Thurgh which treson loste he bothe his yen.
    'Tho redde he me, if that I shal nat lyen,
Of Hercules and of his Dianyre,   725
That caused hym to sette hymself a-fyre.
    'No thyng forgat he, the sorowe [care] and the wo
That Socrates hadde with his wyves two:
How Xantippa caste pisse upon his heed.
This sely man sat stille, as he were deed;   730
He wyped his heed; namoore dorste he seyn,
But, "Er that thonder stinte, comth a reyn!"
    'Of Phasipha, that was the Queen of Crete,
For shrewednesse hym thoughte the tale swete
(Fy! Speke namoore. It is a grisly thing!)   735
Of hire horryble lust and hir lyking.
    'Of Clitermystra, for hire lecherye,
That falsly made hire housbonde for to dye,
He redde it with ful good devocioun.'

Most of the references are self-explanatory. Of those that are not:
Deianira killed Hercules by giving him a robe impregnated with burning
poison; Pasiphae, wife of Minos, had a passion for a bull and gave birth to
the monstrous Minotaur; and Clytemnestra murdered her husband
Agamemnon in his bath so that she could be with her lover.

'But now to get to the point of why I told you,
That I was beaten for a book, certainly.
One night Jankin, who was my 'lord and master',
Was reading in his book, as he sat by the fire,
Of the first woman, Eve, who, by her wickedness,   715
Brought all mankind to wretchedness,
Which was the reason why Jesus Christ himself was slain,
Who, with His heart's blood, redeemed our sins.
Well, here expressly stated, may you find
That woman was the ruin of all mankind.   720
    'Then he read to me about how Samson lost his hair,
His lover cut it with her scissors while he was sleeping;
Through which act of treason he lost both his eyes.
    'Then read he out, if I am not to lie,
About Hercules, and his Deianira   725
Who caused him to go and set himself on fire.
    'He omitted nothing of the suffering and misery
That Socrates had with his two wives:
How Xantippe threw piss upon his head.
This hapless man sat still, as if he were dead;   730
He wiped his head, and no more dare he say
Than, "Before the thunder ceases comes the rain."
    'Of Pasiphae, the Queen of Crete,
Out of perversity, he found that story of female wickedness a sweet
example
(Fie! Say no more. It is an awful thing!),   735
Of her horrible lust and sexual desire.
    'Of Clytemnestra, for her lechery,
Who caused her husband's murder by treachery,
He read all these with the greatest devotion.'

'He tolde me, eek, for what occasioun   740
Amphiorax at Thebes loste his lyf.
Myn housbonde hadde a legende of his wyf,
Eriphilem, that for an ouche of gold
Hath prively unto the Grekes told
Wher that hir housbonde hidde him in a place,   745
For which he hadde at Thebes sory grace.
      'Of Lyvia tolde he me, and of Lucye.
They bothe made hir housbondes for to dye:
That oon for love, that oother was for hate.
Lyvia hir housbonde, on an even late,   750
Empoysoned hath, for that she was his fo;
Lucia, likerous, loved hire housbonde so
That, for he sholde alwey upon hire thynke,
She yaf hym swich a manere love-drynke
That he was deed er it were by the morwe: 755
And thus algates housbondes han sorwe.
      'Thanne tolde he me how oon Latumyus
Compleyned unto his felawe Arrius
That in his gardin growed swich a tree
On which, he seyde, how that his wyves thre   760
Hanged hemself for herte despitus.
"O leeve brother!" quod this Arrius,
"Yif me a plante of thilke blissed tree,
And in my gardin planted shal it bee."'

All references are self-explanatory. The story of Arrius and the tree is
really very funny.

'He told me, too, just when and how   740
Amphiaraus at Thebes lost his life.
My husband had a story of his wife
Eriphyle who, for a brooch of gold,
In secrecy told the Greeks
Where her husband's hiding place was,   745
As a result of which he met with ill luck at Thebes.
    'Of Livia and Lucia he told me,
For both of them caused the deaths of their husbands:
The one for love, the other killed for hate.
Livia made her husband drink some poison   750
Late one evening because she hated him;
Lucia, full of lust, loved her husband so much
That, to make him think constantly upon her,
She gave him a love potion of such a kind,
That he was dead before the next morning: 755
And husbands thus in every way come to sorrow.
    'Then did he tell how one Latumius
Complained to his close friend Arrius
That in his garden grew a particular tree
From which, he said, his three wives   760
Had hanged themselves out of spiteful hatred.
"O dear brother," Arrius said.
"Give me a cutting of that same blessed tree
And it shall be planted in my garden!"'

'Of latter date, of wyves hath he red   765
That somme han slayn hir housbondes in hir bed
And lete hir lecchour dighte hire al the night,
Whan that the corps lay in the floor upright,
And somme han dryve nayles in hir brayn
Whil that they slepte, and thus they han hem slayn,   770
Somme han hem yeve poysoun in hire drinke.
    'He spak moore harm than herte may bithinke,
And therwithal he knew of mo proverbes
Than in this world ther growen gras or herbes.
"Bet is," quod he, "thyn habitacioun   775
Be with a leoun or a foul dragoun,
Than with a womman usinge for to chyde."
"Bet is," quod he, "hye in the roof abyde,
Than with an angry wyf doun in the hous.
They been so wikked and contrarious,   780
They haten that hir housbondes loven ay."
He seyde, "A womman cast hir shame away,
Whan she cast of hir smok;" and forthermo,
"A fair womman, but she be chaast also,
Is lyk a gold ryng in a sowes nose."   785
    'Who wolde wene, or who wolde suppose,
The wo that in myn herte was, and pyne?
And whan I saugh he wolde nevere fyne
To reden on this cursed book al night,
Al sodeynly thre leves have I plight   790
Out of his book, right as he radde, and eke
I with my fest so took hym on the cheke
That in oure fyr he fil bakward adoun.'

The climax of the story of Alison and Jankin comes in ripping out of
pages from his book. Earlier, the Wife says that she "rente out of his book a
leef" (635 and 667), but a little exaggeration adds to the drama here. Notice
also that the Wife changes from the simple past tense, "whan I *saugh* he
wolde" (788) to the present perfect, "thre leves *have I plight* / Out of his
book" (790-1), which makes her action much more immediate and dramatic.

    Lines 775-6 refer to Ecclesiasticus xxv 16: "There is no head above the
head of a serpent; and there is no wrath above the wrath of an enemy," and to

'Of wives of more recent times he also read,   765
How some had slain their husbands in their bed
And allowed their lovers to make love to them all night
While their husband's corpse lay on his back upon the floor.
And some had driven nails into their brains
While their husbands slept and in this way killed them.   770
And some had given them poison in their drink.
    'He told more evil than the heart can think.
And in addition he knew of more proverbs
Than in this world there grow grasses or plants.
"Better it is," he said, "to live with   775
A lion wild or horrible dragon,
Than with a woman who will always be nagging."
"It is better," he said, "to live high in the roof space
Than down in the house with a bitter wife.
They are so wicked and argumentative,   780
They always hate the thing their husband loves."
He said, "A woman throws away her modesty
When she throws off her smock," and added,
"A fair woman, unless she is also chaste.
Is like a ring of gold in a pig's nose."   785
    'Who would think or who would imagine
What misery and pain in my heart?
And when I saw he would never leave off,
His reading in this cursed book at night,
Suddenly, three pages of it I have torn   790
Out of his book, just as he was reading; and then
I hit him on the cheek with my fist
So that he fell right down backwards into our fire.'

Proverbs xxi 19: "It is better to dwell in the wilderness, than with a
contentious and an angry woman." Lines 778-9 refer to Proverbs xxi 9: "It is
better to dwell in a corner of the housetop, than with a brawling woman in a
wide house." Lines 784-5 refer to Proverbs xi 22: "As a jewel of gold in a
swine's snout, so is a fair woman which is without discretion" where the
reference is to a foolish woman not to an unchaste woman (King James).

'And he up stirte as dooth a wood leoun,
And with his fest he smoot me on the heed,   795
That in the floor I lay as I were deed.
And whan he saugh how stille that I lay,
He was agast, and wolde han fled his way,
Til atte laste out of my swogh I breyde.
    '"O! hastow slayn me, false theef?" I seyde,   800
"And for my land thus hastow mordred me?
Er I be deed, yet wol I kisse thee."
    'And neer he cam and kneled faire adoun,
And seyde, "Deere suster Alisoun,
As help me God! I shal thee nevere smyte.   805
That I have doon, it is thyself to wyte.
Foryeve it me, and that I thee biseke!"
    'And yet eftsoones I hitte hym on the cheke,
And seyde, "Theef, thus muchel am I wreke;
Now wol I dye, I may no lenger speke."   810
    'But atte laste, with muchel care and wo,
We fille acorded by us selven two.
He yaf me al the bridel in myn hond,
To han the governance of hous and lond,
And of his tonge, and of his hond also -   815
And made hym brenne his book anon right tho.'

The Wife introduces humor in her description of how she bested Jankin
and snatched victory from the jaws of defeat. The first clue is the description
of her lying "in the floor I lay as I were deed" (796) which indicates that she
immediately pretended to be more seriously hurt than she was. Jankin is so
aghast at what he thinks he has done that he panics and considers running
away, but to prevent him from doing so, Alison stages a well-timed, gradual
recovery of her senses. Then, she accuses him of the very kind of murder
about which he has just been reading to her, and pathetically asks for one kiss
before she dies as a token of her forgiveness and continuing love for him.
Jankin completely falls for it. He kneels gently by his wife's side, calls her
"suster" (804) acknowledging her as a fellow Christian in what he is
convinced are her last moments (Cigman 162), promises never to hit her
again, and begs for her forgiveness. He has, however, made a grave error in
still insisting that his wife is responsible for what has just happened, "That I
have doon, it is thyself to wyte" (806). Nevertheless, what happens next is

'Then he jumped up like a raging lion,
And with his fist he struck me on the head,   795
So that I lay on the floor as if I were dead.
And when he saw how still I lay,
He was horrified and thought about running away,
Until finally I started to recover from my faint.
      '"Oh, have you slain me, you criminal?" I said,   800
"And for my land have you thus murdered me?
Yet before I die, I will kiss you."
      'He came close to me and gently knelt down,
And said: "O my dear sister Alison,
So help me God, I shall never strike you again;   805
What I have done, it was your own fault.
Forgive me, that is all I beseech of you!"
      'And thereupon I once again hit him on the cheek,
And said: "Thief, so much vengeance do I take!
Now will I die; I can no longer speak!"   810
      'But eventually, after much care and woe,
We came to an understanding between ourselves.
He put the bridle reins into my hand
To have the control of the house and the land;
And of his speech and of his actions also -   815
And I made him burn his book, then and there.'

almost as big a shock to the reader as it certainly is to Jankin: she hits him in
the face a second time. This time, Jankin does not retaliate because he has
been fooled into thinking that this is the last action of a dying woman!

Exactly how the two become reconciled is not explained, but it is clear
that Jankin eventually gives his wife complete freedom to go where she
wishes, to control the household and estate finances, and even to manage his
own conduct and speech. Of course, her first act is to make him burn that
anti-feminist book! But after that, as we shall see, there is nothing further to
fight about. Once he stops telling her what to do, Alison is perfectly happy to
do it!

'And whan that I hadde geten unto me,
By maistrie, al the soveraynetee,
And that he seyde, "Myn owene trewe wyf,
Do as thee lust the terme of al thy lyf;   820
Keep thyn honour, and keep eek myn estaat."
     'After that day we hadden never debaat.
God helpe me so, I was to hym as kynde
As any wyf from Denmark unto Ynde,
And also trewe, and so was he to me.   825
I prey to God, that sit in magestee,
So blesse his soule for His mercy deere.
Now wol I seye my tale, if ye wol heere.'

Line 820 carries a sad irony. When Jankin promises his wife that she shall do just as she wishes for the rest of her life, he must assume that (given the twenty-year age gap between them) he will outlive her. One difference between the 'real life' story of Alison and Jankin and the fairy tale story of the knight and the loathly lady is that in the latter the couple has a long life together and 'live happily ever after.' Life in the real medieval world was shorter and more precarious than it is today.

The resolution of the story of the Wife and Jankin is perfunctory, but the reader does not doubt that once he has ceased to enforce his male supremacy she is as dutiful a wife as he could wish to have, or her sincerity in expressing her love for her late husband. As a story teller, Alison is clearly less interested in describing peace than she is in describing conflict.

Wetherbee comments that "it is a measure of the limitation of the Wife's situation that she never attains the point of envisioning an alternative to the stereotypical view" of the place of women within marriage and society (73) and is, like the Prioress and the Second Nun, "incapable of imagining an existence freed from authoritarian social and religious strictures" (74). Perhaps it is splitting hairs to refine this just a little. Both the *Prologue* and the *Tale* prove that Alison can *envisage* an alternative, but in neither can she (or at least in neither does she) *describe* it in any detail.

'And when I had thus gathered unto me.
Through determination, the entire sovereignty,
And he had said: "My own true wedded wife,
Do as you please for the rest of your life,   820
Take responsibility for your own honor and for my worldly affairs."
    'After that day, we never had an argument.
So God help me, I was as kind to him
As any wife from Denmark unto India,
And also faithful, and so was he to me.   825
I pray to God, who sits in majesty,
To bless his soul, out of His dear mercy!
Now will I tell my tale, if you will hear.'

Ladies carding and spinning wool. After having great importance in
the portrait of the Wife of Bath, no mention is made of her cloth
making in her Prologue. (Engraving 1891 based on medieval
painting. Wikimedia Commons. Public domain.)

Biholde the wordes bitwene the Somonour and the Frere wordes.

The Frere lough, whan he hadde herd al this.
'Now dame,' quod he, 'so have I joye or blis,   830
This is a long preamble of a tale!'
    And whan the Somonour herde the Frere gale,
'Lo,' quod the Somonour, 'Goddes armes two!
A frere wol entremette him everemo.
Lo, goode men, a flye and eek a frere   835
Wol falle in every dissh and eek mateere.
What spekestow of preambulacioun?
What! Amble, or trotte, or pees, or go sit doun!
Thou lettest oure disport in this manere.'
    'Ye, woltow so, sire Somonour?' quod the Frere.   840
'Now, by my feith, I shal, er that I go,
Telle of a somonour swich a tale or two,
That alle the folk shal laughen in this place.'
    'Now elles, Frere, I bishrewe thy face,'
Quod this Somonour, 'and I bishrewe me,   845
But if I telle tales two or thre
Of freres, er I come to Sidingborne,
That I shal make thyn herte for to morne,
For wel I woot thy pacience is gon.'
    Oure Hooste cryde, 'Pees! and that anon!'   850
And seyde, 'Lat the womman telle hire tale.
Ye fare as folk that dronken ben of ale.
Do, dame, telle forth youre tale, and that is best.'
    'Al redy, sire,' quod she, 'right as yow lest -
If I have licence of this worthy frere.'   855
    'Yis, dame,' quod he, 'tel forth, and I wol heere.'

In *The General Prologue*, the frame story of the thirty pilgrims going to
Canterbury is developed by their exchanges along the way between (and
sometimes in the middle of) the tales. The developing dynamic between the
pilgrims, as here in the argument between the Friar and the Summoner, will
influence the stories that they tell. This degree of dramatic realism is
something is quite new in medieval literature.
    Recall that the original concept was for each pilgrim to tell two tales on
the way to Canterbury and two on the return journey to London.

Listen to the altercation between the Summoner and the Friar.

The Friar laughed when he had heard all this.
'Now lady,' said he, 'as I may have joy or bliss   830
This is a long prelude to a tale!'
    And when the Summoner heard this Friar complain,
'Oh,' said the Summoner, 'by God's two arms!
A friar will always be interfering.
Behold, good men, a housefly and a friar   835
Will fall into every dish and everything else that is going on.
Why do you complain of preluding?
What! Push off, shut up, or go and sit down!
You are ruining our pleasure with your griping.'
    'So, is that what you feel, sir Summoner?' said the Friar.   840
'Now by my faith I will, before I go,
Tell of a summoner such a tale, or two,
That all the folk shall laugh who are in this place.'
    'Do as you please, Friar, I curse your face,'
Replied this Summoner, 'and the Devil take me too   845
If I do not tell two or three tales,
Of friars before I get to Sittingbourne,
That certainly will give you cause to be sorry,
For well I know you have already lost your temper.'
    Our Host cried out, 'Now shut up! This instant!'   850
And said, 'Let the woman tell her tale.
You act like people who are drunk on ale.
Do, my lady, tell your tale, and that is best.'
    'All ready, sir,' said she, 'just as you wish -
If I have the permission of this worthy Friar.'   855
    'Yes, my lady,' said he, 'tell on, and I shall listen.'

Cigman notices that the Wife is unnaturally "docile" in the face of the Friar's outburst of criticism, but points to her jibe at the Friar when she says, "If I have licence of this worthy frere" (855) seeing a sly reference, which would have been clear to all of the other pilgrims, to the fact that the Friar himself has a licence to go around begging in a particular district (163).

The argument between the Friar and the Summoner is really bitter, with the Summoner (an official of the Church courts but probably not himself a cleric) expressing himself very bluntly indeed. His blasphemy on line 833 is particularly shocking.

Chapter 5: *The Wife of Bath's Tale*

In th' olde dayes of the King Arthour,
Of which that Britons speken greet honour,
Al was this land full-fill'd of fayerye:
The Elf-Queene, with hir joly compaignye,   860
Daunced ful ofte in many a grene mede.
This was the olde opinion, as I rede
(I speke of manye hundred yeres ago),
But now kan no man se none elves mo,
For now the grete charitee and prayers   865
Of lymytours and othere hooly frères,
That serchen every lond and ev'ry streem,
As thikke as motes in the sonne-beem,
Blessinge halles, chambres, kichenes, boures,
Citees, burghes, castels, hye toures,   870
Thropes, bernes, shipnes, dayeryes;
This maketh that ther ben no fayeryes.
For ther as wont to walken was an elf
Ther walketh now the lymytour himself
In undermeles and in morweninges,   875
And seyth his Matyns and his hooly thinges
As he gooth in his lymytacioun.
Wommen may go saufly up and doun.
In every bussh, or under every tree,
Ther is noon oother incubus but he,   880
And he ne wol doon hem but dishonor!

In the only poem by Chaucer that even mentions King Arthur, the narrator sets the scene in an England from which the fairies have not yet been banished by spreading Christianity; where fairy magic still exists; where the "Elf-Queene" rules (860); and where Arthur's power is merely temporal. From the moment of the knight's crime, supernatural forces, controlled by the Elf-Queen, manipulate events to ensure that the knight learns his lesson. Perhaps the old hag who the knight meets is the Elf-Queen herself.

The Wife's first digression contrasts the world of the tale and with the England of the present, where the all-male Church has radically changed the way women are viewed in society. Particularly, Alison attacks the corruption of friars. The Wife is satirical: her apparent praise of the changes in society

In the olden days of King Arthur,
Of whom the Britons speak with great reverence,
This land was all filled full with fairy magic:
The Fairy Queen, with her merry company,   860
Danced frequently in many a green meadow.
This was the old belief, as I read;
I speak of many hundred years ago.
But today no man can see elves anymore,
For now we see the great charity and prayers   865
Of those friars who are licensed beggars and of other holy friars,
That search out every acre of land and every stream,
As thick as specks of dust in the sun's beams,
Blessing halls, chambers, kitchens, bedrooms,   869
Cities, boroughs [towns with a royal charter], castles, high towers,
Villages, barns, stables, dairies -
This is the reason that there are no more fairies.
For where an elf was accustomed to walk
Now there walks the licensed begging friar himself
In the mornings and the afternoons,   875
Saying his matins and devotional prayers
As he progresses through his assigned begging district.
Now women may go safely up and down.
In every bush or under every tree
There is no other incubus [evil spirit that copulates with women in
their sleep] but the friar,   880
And he will not do them harm - except by bringing them shame and
dishonor!

wrought by the ubiquitous friars and of the protection they have brought to women's virtue is bitterly ironic.

If we accept the idea of *The Canterbury Tales* as a drama, then the attack is intended for the ears of Friar Hubert who has just had the temerity to complain about the length of the Wife's *Prologue*. He is described in *The General Prologue* as a limiter, "the beste beggere in his hous" (252), who makes much more by begging in his district than he pays for his begging licence, "His purchas was wel bettre than his rente" (258). Hubert is also sexually promiscuous carrying seductions gifts. "His tipet was ay farsed ful of knives / And pinnes, for to yeven faire wives" (233-4), and arranges marriages for the young maidens who he gets pregnant, "He hadde maad ful many a marriage / Of yonge wommen at his owene cost" (212-3).

And so bifel that this King Arthour
Hadde in his hous a lusty bacheler,
That on a day cam rydinge fro river;
And happed that, allone as he was born,   885
He saugh a mayde walkinge him biforn,
Of which mayde anon, maugree hir heed,
By verray force, he rafte hire maydenheed;
For which oppressioun was swich clamour
And swich pursute unto the King Arthour,   890
That dampned was this knyght for to be deed,
By cours of lawe, and sholde han lost his heed
(Paraventure, swich was the statut tho)
But that the Queene and other ladyes mo,
So longe preyeden the King of grace   895
Til he his lyf him graunted in the place,
And yaf him to the Queene al at hir wille,
To chese wheither she wolde hym save or spille.

The knight in question is a young man "who has not yet attained the status - through maturity, land and vassals - to display his own banner and who therefore follows the banner of one who has [his father]" (Cigman 165). The description is very similar to that of the Squire in *The General Prologue* whose is, "A lover and a lusty bachelor ... / So hot he loved that, while night told her tale, / He slept no more than does a nightingale" (80-98 Author's modernization).

Line 893 refers to the Statute of 1285 which made rape a capital offense in England. The knight's crime is integral to the theme of both the *Prologue* and *Tale* because "[t]he act of rape "symbolizes the ultimate mastery of woman by man" (Cigman 11). No punches are pulled in the description of his crime: the girl is alone and defenseless; it is stated that she is a virgin; the knight acts impulsively without a moment's hesitation; and finally the violence of the attack is emphasized. The adjective "verray" stresses this, reminding us that the adjective "lusty" clearly has connotations of sexual appetite.

The theme of male dominance is clear both in the innocent maiden's helplessness and in King Author's ultimate legal authority. However, the power of women is also evident, for the Queen and her ladies-in-waiting appear to have very little difficulty in bending the King to their will. Thus, it is not power that the court women lack but *officially sanctioned power*. The law places all authority in the man; to achieve equality women need to have their rights legally recognized.

104

And so it fell out that this King Arthur
Had in his court a virile young knight,
Who one day came riding from hawking by the side of the river,
And it happened that, alone as he rode along,   885
He saw a virgin maiden walking ahead of him,
Which maiden immediately, despite all that she could do to resist,
By brute force, he robbed her of her maidenhead [i.e. raped her];
For which violation there was such an outcry
And such appeal to King Arthur for justice   890
That this knight was condemned to death,
By course of law, and should have lost his head
(For that was according the statute then in place)
Had not the Queen and other ladies as well
Persistently begged the King to show him mercy   895
Until he granted him his life on the spot,
And placed his fate in the will of the Queen,
To decide whether she would him save or have him put to death.

The modern reader expects the girl to reappear in the story, but this is
actually the last we hear of her. Does she get pregnant? Do her parents throw
her out? We do not know. Looked at from the perspective of the twentieth
century novel, this is deeply unsatisfactory. Of course, it could be argued that
in the fourteenth century people from the girl's class (she's obviously not a
court lady) were pretty expendable; the writer was only concerned with
nobles. On the other hand, she could be regarded as a symbol; that is, one
woman who is all women. Looked at in this way, the fate of the knight
represents justice for all women, including the maiden. It is made perfectly
clear that, by his crime, the knight ironically loses all control of his fate
which is placed in the hands of women, "[Arthur] yaf him to the Queene al at
hir wille, / To chese wheither she wolde him save or spille" (897-7).

A legal record of 1380, when Chaucer would have been approaching 40,
states that Cecelia Chaumpaigne, the daughter of a London baker, agrees to
release Geoffrey Chaucer from all further legal action concerning "*de raptu
meo.*" The phrase probably means abduction rather than sexual assault, but it
appears that Chaucer, or his representative, was willing to pay £10 per year
to Cecelia to settle the matter out of court. That's as much as we know about
this incident, and as much as we are ever likely to know. It has been
suggested, however, that *The Wife of Bath's Tale* was written by Chaucer as
an act of atonement for his crime. We sall never know.

The Queene thankede the King with al hir myght,
And after this thus spak she to the knyght, 900
Whan that she saugh hir tyme, upon a day.
  "Thou standest yet," quod she, "in swich array
That of thy lyf yet hastow no suretee.
I grante thee lyf, if thou kanst tellen me
What thyng is it that wommen moost desyren. 905
Be war, and keep thy nekke-boon from yren!
And if thou kanst nat tellen it anon,
Yet wool I yeve thee leve for to gon
A twelf-month and a day, to seche and leere
An answere suffisant in this mateere, 910
And suretee wol I han, er that thou pace,
Thy body for to yelden in this place."
  Wo was this knyght, and sorwefully he syketh;
But what! He may nat do al as hym lyketh.
And, at the laste, he chees hym for to wende, 915
And come agayn, right at the yeres ende,
With swich answere as God wolde hym purveye;
And taketh his leve, and wendeth forth his weye.
  He seketh every hous and every place
Where as he hopeth for to fynde grace 920
To lerne what thyng wommen loven moost,
But he ne koude arryven in no coost
Wher as he myghte fynde in this mateere
Two creatures accordinge in-feere.

The description of the knight being brought to justice in a court of women with the Queen presiding is clearly a reference to the Courts of Love presided over (in contemporary romantic literature, though not in fact) by the beautiful Queen Eleanor of Aquitaine. On many levels, the Tale will function as wish fulfillment for the Wife.

Walter Map concludes *The Letter of Valerius to Rufinus Against Marriage* with the assertion that women simply cannot say, "No." He claims that, though a woman may reject a suitor, she will always do so with some tantalizing hint of encouragement; no woman will ever give a wooer a final refusal. Although Map's aim is to show how morally inferior women are, his argument leads directly to the belief that when a woman says "No" (as the maiden by the river certainly did), she actually means "Yes."

The Queen thanked the King sincerely,
And afterwards she spoke these words to the knight,   900
One day when she saw the right opportunity.
    "You still stand," she said, "in such a situation,
That you have no certainty of your life.
I grant that you shall live on condition that you can tell me
What thing it is that women most desire.   905
Be prudent, and keep your neck from the blade!
And if you cannot give me the answer right away,
I will give you leave to go
A twelvemonth and a day, to search for and learn
A satisfactory answer on this subject,   910
And you will give me a pledge before you go,
To surrender your body in this place."
    This knight was wretched, and he sighs sorrowfully;
But what can he do? He is not free to act as he pleases.
And finally he chooses to go on his travels   915
And return, exactly at the year's end,
With such an answer as God will provide him with;
And so he takes his leave, and sets off on his way.
    He seeks out every house and every place
Where he has hopes to have the good fortune   920
To learn what thing it is that women love most,
But he never could discover any region
Where he might find in this puzzle
Two people agreeing with one another.

On line 913, the verb tense changes from the simple past tense ("Queene thanked ... she saugh hir tyme") to the historic present tense, that is, the present tense is used to describe actions and feelings which, it has already been established, happened long ago. Thus, the knight, "syketh ... may nat do ... chees hym " (913-5). The effect of the change is to draw the reader into the story, and specifically to encourage the reader to identify with the knight's mysterious and seemingly impossible quest.

Somme seyde wommen loven best richesse,   925
Somme seyde honour, somme seyde jolynesse,
Somme riche array, somme seyden lust abedde,
And ofte-tyme to be wydwe and wedde.
    Somme seyde that oure hertes been moost esed
Whan that we been yflatered and yplesed.   930
He gooth ful ny the sothe, I wol nat lye.
A man shal wynne us best with flaterye,
And with attendance and with bisynesse
Been we ylymed, bothe moore and lesse.
    And somme seyen that we loven best   935
For to be free and do right as us lest,
And that no man repreve us of oure vyce,
But seye that we be wyse and no thyng nyce.
For trewely, ther is noon of us alle,
If any wyght wol clawe us on the galle,   940
That we nel kike, for he seith us sooth.
Assay, and he shal fynde it that so dooth;
For, be we never so vicious withinne,
We wol been holden wyse and clene of sinne.
    And somme seyen that greet delyt han we   945
For to been holden stable and eek secree,
And in o purpos stedefastly to dwelle,
And nat biwreye thyng that men us telle -
But that tale is nat worth a rake-stele!
Pardee! We wommen konne no thyng hele: 950
Witnesse on Myda - wol ye heere the tale?

The Wife of Bath has managed to keep to the convention of the third
person narrator since beginning the actual narrative on line 882. The
temptation to editorialize, however, proves too much: on lines 931-4, she
speaks in her own voice commenting on the answer that women like to be
flattered and pampered, which she enthusiastically rates as a near miss; on
lines 938-44, she finds truth in the answer that women want not to be
reproached for their faults (compare 661-3); and, beginning on line 948,
Alison considers the answer that women want to be regarded as able to keep
a secret so very wide of the mark that it leads her off at a tangent onto the
tale of Midas' wife. Clearly, the question which the knight has been set is not
merely of narrative interest (i.e. necessary to the plot). On the contrary, it is
one in which Alison has a passionate personal interest.

Some said women love wealth best,   925
Some said honorable reputation, some said lightheartedness,
Some rich clothing, some said a vigorous sex-life,
And frequently to be widowed and remarried.
     Some said that our women's hearts are most eased
When we are flattered and pampered.   930
That answer comes very near the truth, I will not deny it.
A man shall win us best with flattery,
And with attentions and with solicitude
We are caught, every one of us great and small.
     And some say that we love best   935
To be free and to do just as we please,
And that no man reproach us for our faults,
But swear that we are wise and not at all foolish.
For truly there is not one of us women,
Who, if any one will scratch us on the sore spot,   940
Will not kick out, because he tells us the truth.
Try it, and any man that does so shall find it true;
For, be we never so vicious within,
We want to be considered wise and clear of sin.
     And some say that we have great delight   945
To be considered sensible, and also able to keep a secret,
And to remain steadfast in one purpose,
And not reveal secrets that men tell us -
But that tale is not worth a rake handle!
By God! We women can hide nothing: 950
Witness the fate of Midas - Will you hear the tale?

     The key to the narrator's involvement is in the shifting verb tenses. The initial answers that the knight receives are all in the past tense ("seyde' but they gradually transition to the present tense ("seyen"). The Wife has stepped beyond her story into what people say about women in her own day. Thus, the past tense of, "Whan that we been yflatered" (930), becomes the present tense of, "We wol been holden wise" (944). From this point on, the narrator completely identifies herself with the subject of the enquiry so that the plural noun ""wommen" is replaced by the plural first person pronouns "we" and "us."

     The catalogue of opinions recalls the list of accusations that the Wife attributed to her husbands. They are both familiar stereotypes, all of which underestimate the intellect and determination of women.

Ovyde, amonges othere thynges smale,
Seyde Myda hadde, under his longe heres,
Growinge upon his heed two asses eres,
The whiche vyce he hydde as he best mighte   955
Ful subtilly from every mannes sighte,
That, save his wyf, ther wiste of it namo.
He loved hire moost, and trusted hire also;
He preyede hire that to no creature
She sholde tellen of his disfigure.   960
     She swoor him, "Nay." For al this world to wynne,
She nolde do that vileynye or synne,
To make hir housbonde han so foul a name.
She nolde nat telle it for hir owene shame.
But nathelees, hir thoughte that she dyde   965
That she so longe sholde a conseil hyde.
Hir thoughte it swal so soore aboute hir herte
That nedely som word hire moste asterte,
And sith she dorste telle it to no man,
Doun to a mareys faste by she ran   970
(Til she cam, there hir herte was afyre),
And as a bitore bombleth in the myre,
She leyde hir mouth unto the water doun.
     "Biwreye me nat, thou water, with thy soun,"
Quod she, "to thee I telle it and namo;   975
Myn housbonde hath longe asses erys two!
Now is myn herte al hool; now is it oute.
I myghte no lenger kepe it, out of doute."
     Heere may ye se, thogh we a tyme abyde,
Yet out it moot; we kan no conseil hyde.   980
The remenant of the tale if ye wol heere,
Redeth Ovyde, and ther ye may it leere.

The Wife of Bath freely adapts Ovid's tale for her own narrative
purposes. In the original, it is Midas' barber who is sworn to secrecy about
the ears but who cannot resist speaking the truth to a hole in the ground. Out
of this hole eventually reeds grow, and when the wind rustles them they
repeat the sound of the barber's words.
     It seems inconsistent that someone so assertive of the claims of women

Ovid, among other short tales,
Said that Midas had, beneath his long hair,
Growing upon his head a pair of ass's ears,
Which deformity he hid, as well as he could,   955
Very artfully from every person's sight,
And no one except his wife knew anything about it.
He loved her most, and also trusted her;
And he entreated her that
She should tell no one about his disfigurement.   960
     She swore to him that even to gain the whole world
She would not do such a shameful, sinful action
Which would cause her husband to have so foul a reputation;
Neither would she tell it because of her own sense of deep shame.
Nevertheless, she thought she would have died   965
If she had to hide the secret for a long time;.
The burden of it seemed to swell so painfully in her heart
That some word must inevitably burst from her mouth.,
And since she dared not tell it to any human,
Down to a marsh that lay nearby she ran,   970
Till she came there her heart was all aflame,
And, as a bittern [a marsh bird] booms in the wetland,
She bent her mouth low down to the water.
     "Do not betray me, O water with your sound,'"
Said she, "I tell it to none else but you: 975
My husband has two long ears like asses have!
Now is my heart at quite well again, since that is out;
I could no longer have kept it a secret, of that there is no doubt."
     Here may you see, though we women may delay for a time,
We just cannot keep a secret; it must come out.   980
If you would hear the remainder of this story,
Read Ovid: learn about it there.

to equality should tell a story which almost glorifies a wife's frailty, but never in her *Prologue* does the Wife claim that women are perfect; she merely wants for women what she wants for herself, which is, to be accepted *for what she is*. Notice also that the story illustrates the monumental stupidity of men, and that Midas certainly comes out worst in the end.

This knyght, of which my tale is specially,
Whan that he saugh he mighte nat come therby
(This is to seye, what wommen love moost)   985
Withinne his brest ful sorweful was the goost,
But hoom he gooth; he myghte nat sojourne.
The day was come that homward moste he tourney,
And in his wey, it happed hym to ryde,
In al this care, under a forest syde,   990
Wher as he saugh upon a daunce go
Of ladyes foure and twenty, and yet mo;
Toward the whiche daunce he drow ful yerne,
In hope that som wysdom sholde he lerne.
But certeinly, er he cam fully there,   995
Vanysshed was this daunce, he niste where.
No creature saugh he that bar lyf,
Save on the grene, he saugh sittinge a wyf -
A fouler wight ther may no man devyse.
    Agayn the knyght this olde wyf gan ryse,   1000
And seyde, "Sire knyght, heer forth ne lyth no wey.
Tel me what that ye seken, by youre fey.
Paraventure it may the bettre be;
Thise olde folk kan muchel thing," quod she.
    "My leeve mooder," quod this knyght, "certeyn   1005
I nam but deed but if that I kan seyn
What thing it is that wommen moost desyre.
Koude ye me wisse, I wolde wel quyte youre hyre."

At this point in her narrative, the Wife of Bath returns to the theme of
fairy folk with which she began the tale. Line 983 recalls the times in the
Prologue when Alison acknowledges that she has strayed from her subject
(see for example lines 585-6 & 711). Critics often say that the dance of the
young maidens has no role in the narrative. However, the dance is a fairy
dance which echoes the description at the start of the tale, "The Elf-Queene,
with hir joly compaignye, / Daunced ful ofte in many a grene mede" (860-1).
The dancers appear out of nowhere and inexplicably disappear, re-
establishing the presence of fairy magic (and specifically of shape-shifting)
which is central to the tale. The fairies appear to be exploiting the knight's
known weakness for beautiful young women to contrive a meeting with the
ugly old hag, suggesting to the reader that the encounter has some
supernatural purpose.

The knight which my tale chiefly concerns,
When he realized that he could not learn what he wanted to know
(That is, the thing that women most desire),   985
Was saddened in heart and spirit,
But home he goes; he can linger no more.
The day was come when homeward he must turn his way,
And on his journey, it chanced that he should ride,
Oppressed by care, by a forest's side,   990
And there he saw before him, dancing,
Fully twenty-four ladies, maybe even more;
Toward which dance he eagerly drew
In hope that he might learn some wisdom there.
But truly, before he reached the spot,   995
The dancers all vanished, he could not tell where.
No living creature could he see,
Except, sitting on the green grass, was an old woman -
A more hideous person no man could imagine.
    This old woman rose to greet the knight,   1000
And said, "Sir knight, this way leads nowhere.
Tell me what it is that you seek as you are a true knight.
Perhaps everything will turn out for the best;
These ancient folk know a thing or two," said she.
    "My dear good woman," said this knight, "assuredly   1005
I am a dead man unless I can tell, truly,
What thing it is that women most desire.
If you could inform me, I'd reward you handsomely for your trouble."

The meeting also happens at the point where the knight has given up. For a year, he has done everything humanly possible to find an answer, but he has now lost the ability to save his own life. The old woman points to the error of his search when she tells him, "'Sire knyght, heer forth ne lyth no wey'" (1001). The knight offers to reward the woman generously in material terms, "I wolde wel quyte youre hyre" (1008). This is yet another example of a mindset which he needs to overcome: he must go about things in a different way and learn to love and to put his faith in others.

"Plight me thy trouthe, heere in myn hand," quod she,
"The nexte thing that I requere thee,   1010
Thou shalt it do, if it lye in thy might,
And I wol telle it yow, er it be night."
    "Have heer my trouthe," quod the knyght. "I grante."
    "Thanne," quod she, "I dar me wel avante
Thy lyf is sauf, for I wol stonde therby.   1015
Upon my lyf, the Queene wol seye as I.
Lat se which is the proudeste of hem alle
That wereth on a coverchief or a calle
That dar seye nay of that I shal thee teche.
Lat us go forth withouten lenger speche."   1020
    Tho rowned she a pistel in his ere,
And bad hym to be glad and have no fere.

A word is in order on the way in which the knight, the old hag and (later) the Queen speak to each other in this part of the text (1005-1042). The knight first refers to the old woman as "'My leeve mooder'" (1005) which is a polite way of addressing a socially inferior woman who commands a certain respect by virtue of her age. Of course, he addresses the Queen as, "'My lige lady'" (1037), a term which acknowledges his feudal obligation to her as a knight in the service of her husband.

Once he has saluted the old woman, the knight addresses her in the second person plural, "'Koude ye me wisse, I wolde wel quite youre hyre'" (1008), indicating the respectful formality of their relationship. In contrast, the woman immediately uses the second person singular in addressing the knight, "'Plight me thy trouthe ... / The nexte thyng that I requere thee, / Thou shalt it do ... / That dar seye nay of that I shal thee teche'" (1009-1019), a familiar form which is appropriate for an older person addressing a younger, but which also reflects her superior knowledge (she is, after all, a fairy) and the power that it gives her over him. [It is only fair to point to the one exception, "'And I wol telle it yow, er it be night,'" though it hardly negates the general point.] When he presents his answer to the court, the knight addresses the Queen with the second person plural, "This is youre mooste desyr, thogh ye me kille. / Dooth as yow list; I am heer at youre wille'" (1041-2). Once again, this reflects the formality and subservience of his relationship with his liege lady. (Cigman provides a similar analysis.)

Chaucer builds suspense by not telling the reader either what the answer to the to the Queen's question is (see line 1021) and by not allowing either the knight or the reader to know what the old woman's request will be.

"Take my hand and make me a solemn vow," said she,
"That the first thing I ask of you, whatever it may be,   1010
You will perform it if it lies in your power;
And I will give you your answer before night falls."

    "Take my word of honor," said he. "I agree to your conditions."

    "Then," said she, "of this I venture to boast,
Your life is safe, and that is a promise I will stand by.   1015
Upon my life, the Queen will agree with me.
Let's see whether the proudest of them all
That wears upon her hair either a kerchief or a net,
Shall dare say anything to contradict that which I shall teach you.
Let us go now and without longer speech."   1020

    Then she whispered a secret in his ear,
And bade him to be happy and have no fear.

However, there is more than a touch of irony in line 1009 since the woman's request that the knight, "Plight me thy trothe, heere in myn hand" clearly foreshadows the marriage vows. In this way, the reader has the dual pleasures of suspecting, without actually knowing, the nature of the trap into which the knight is blindly walking.

Whan they be comen to the court, this knyght
Seyde he had holde his day, as he hadde hight,
And redy was his answere, as he sayde.   1025
Ful many a noble wyf, and many a mayde,
And many a wydwe, for that they been wyse,
The Queene hirself sittinge as a Justyse,
Assembled been, his answere for to here,
And afterward this knyght was bode appeere.   1030
    To every wight comanded was silence,
And that the knyght sholde telle in audience
What thyng that worldly wommen loven best.
This knyght ne stood nat stille, as doth a best,
But to his questioun anon answerde   1035
With manly voys, that al the court it herde.
    "My lige lady, generally," quod he,
"Wommen desiren to have sovereynetee
As wel over hir housbond as hir love,
And for to been in maistrie him above.   1040
This is youre mooste desyr, thogh ye me kille.
Dooth as yow list; I am heer at youre wille."

The rapist is brought before a court of women: the listing of maidens,
wives and widows with the repetition of the adjective "many" makes the
point that women hold mastery over him. The Wife's comment that widows
are included, "for that they been wyse" (1027) is one of the occasions in the
Tale when we hear the voice of Alison. The pomp of a female court does not,
however, have the effect of humbling the knight because he is supremely
confident that he has the correct answer. Thus, his whole demeanor is manly
and assertive: he speaks confidently in a "manly voys" (1036), and his
answer is concise and to the point.

    There is an irritating arrogance in the way in which the knight presents
himself to the court and particularly how he pretends to place himself in the
Queen's power. Notice that he repeats this idea three times, "'thogh ye me
kille. / Dooth as yow list; I am heer at youre wille'" (1041-2). Ironically, he
is supremely confident of having escaped the power of women by answering
the question at the very moment when he is about to fall even more firmly
into a woman's power. Serves him right!

When they were come into the court, this knight
Said he had kept his word as he had promised,
And was ready with his answer.   1025
There were many noble wives, and many maidens,
And many widows, since they are so wise,
And the Queen herself sitting as chief judge,
Assembled there to hear his answer,
And then the knight was bidden to appear.   1030
        Command was given for every person to be silent,
And that the knight should state before them all
What thing all mortal women love the best.
This knight did not stand dumb as a beast,
But to this question immediately answered   1035
With a manly voice, so that the whole court heard.
        "My liege lady, universally," said he,
"Women desire to have the sovereignty
As well over their husbands as over their lovers,
And to have an authority higher that their man.   1040
This is what you women most desire, though you kill me for saying so.
Do with me as you please; I await your will."

Medieval knight (Karen's
Whimsy. Public domain.)

In al the court ne was ther wyf, ne mayde,
Ne wydwe that contraried that he sayde,
But seyden he was worthy han his lyf.   1045
And with that word up stirte the olde wyf
Which that the knyght saugh sittinge on the grene.
    "Mercy," quod she, "my sovereyn lady Quene!
Er that youre court departe, do me ryght.
I taughte this answere unto the knyght,   1050
For which he plighte me his trouthe there,
The firste thing that I wolde hym requere
He wolde it do, if it lay in his mighte.
Bifore the court thanne preye I thee, sir knyght,"
Quod she, "that thou me take unto thy wyf,   1055
For wel thou woost that I have kept thy lyf.
If I seye fals, sey nay, upon thy fey!"
    This knyght answerde, "Allas and weylawey!
I woot right wel that swich was my biheste.
For Goddes love, as chees a newe requeste!   *Desperation* 1060
Taak al my good and lat my body go."
    "Nay, thanne," quod she, "I shrewe us bothe two!
For thogh that I be foul, and oold, and poore
I nolde for al the metal ne for oore
That under erthe is grave or lyth above,   1065
But if thy wyf I were, and eek thy love."
    "My love?" quod he. "Nay, my dampnacioun!
Allas, that any of my nacioun
Sholde evere so foule disparaged be!"
    But al for noght. The ende is this, that he   1070
Constreyned was: he nedes moste hire wedde,
And taketh his olde wyf, and gooth to bedde.

Line 1047 seems a little redundant, even if we recall that most people
experienced these stories by hearing them read rather than by reading them.
It is, however, important for the narrator to remind the reader at this point
that the old woman is more than she appears to be. The color green associates
her with woodland spirits, foreshadowing that the supernatural will play
some part in the climax of the tale.
    The knight is caught in a classic Catch-22: as a nobleman, it is
dishonorable for him to marry a woman from the laboring class (particularly

In all the court, there was neither wife, nor maid,
Nor widow who contradicted what he said,
But all decided that he was worthy of living.   1045
And with that verdict up jumped the old wife
Whom he had seen sitting on the green.
    "Mercy," cried she, "my sovereign lady Queen!
Before you dismiss the court, give me justice.
I taught this answer to the knight,   1050
For which he did vow to me, right there,
That the first thing I should require him to do
He would perform it, if it lay in his power.
Before the court, then, I pray you, sir knight,"
Said she, "that you will take me for your wife,   1055
For well you know that I have saved your life.
If this is not the truth, say nay and swear upon your honor!"
    This knight replied, "Alas and woe is me!
I know well enough that I so promised,
But for the love of God I beg you make a new request.   1060
Take all my wealth, but let my body go."
    "Nay then," said she, "I curse us both if I do!
For though I may be ugly and old and poor,
I will not, for all the metal and all the ore
That is hidden in the earth or lies above it,   1065
Be anything other than your wife and your true love."
    "My love?" cried he, "no, my damnation!
Alas! That anyone of my birth and lineage
Should ever be so foully degraded!"
    But it was all for nothing. The end is that he   1070
Was no longer free: he needs must marry her,
And take his old woman and go to bed.

an old and ugly one), but he has given his word to do what the old woman
asks, and as a nobleman it would be more dishonorable for him to go back on
his oath. Remembering the knight's initial crime, the narrative presents him
as getting exactly what he deserves: he has unwittingly placed himself
entirely in the power of a woman. Line 1061 parallels Alison's statement
"Thou shalt nat bothe, thogh that thou wert wood, / Be maister of my body
and my good; / The oon thou shalt forgo, maugree thyne yen" (313-5). Both
she and the knight learn that they must give up control of both to be loved.

Now wolden som men seye, paraventure,
That for my necligence I do no cure
To tellen yow the joye and al th' array   1075
That at the feste was that ilke day.
To which thyng shortly answeren I shal:
I seye ther nas no joye ne feste at al.
Ther nas but hevynesse and muche sorwe,
For prively he wedded hire on morwe,   1080
And al day after hidde hym as an oule,
So wo was him, his wyf looked so foule.
    Greet was the wo the knyght hadde in his thoght,
Whan he was with his wyf abedde y-broght;
He walweth, and he turneth to and fro.   1085
His olde wyf lay smylinge everemo,
And seyde, "O deere housbonde, benedicitee!
Fareth every knyght thus with his wyf as ye?
Is this the lawe of King Arthoures hous?
Is every knyght of his so dangerous?   1090
    "I am youre owene love and youre wyf;
I am she which that saved hath [eek] youre lyf,
And, certes, yet ne dide I yow nevere unright;
Why fare ye thus with me this firste night?   *imperative*
Ye faren lyk a man had lost his wit.   1095
What is my gilt? For Goddes love, tel me it,
And it shal been amended, if I may."   *acquiescing*

lots of question

What is very noticeable here is the contrast in mood between the knight
and his new bride. While the knight is in the depths of despair and does
everything to postpone the terrible moment when he is expected to
consummate the marriage by having sex with the old woman, she is calmness
personified, smiling at his discomfiture. She is in control of the situation.

The old woman also obviously enjoys playing the role of naive, innocent
victim who has not the faintest idea what could be wrong. Her questions have
a mocking tone. At the same time, subtly, but forcefully, she is establishing
that morally she is in the right: the knight owes her his life; she loves him
truly; and she has never done him any wrong. Each of these assertions is
unanswerably true. The fault is not with the old woman but with the knight,
who got himself into this mess by raping an innocent maiden and needs to
change the mindset that allowed him to do it.

Now, perhaps, some men would say here,
That, through careless negligence, I am not taking the trouble
To tell you of the joy and all the pomp   1075
That was seen at the wedding feast that same day.
I shall make a brief answer to this charge:
I say, there was neither joy nor celebration at all.
There was only despondency and grievous sorrow,
For he was married privately on the following morning,   1080
And subsequently, all day, he hid himself like an owl
So sad was he because his old wife looked so hideous.
     Great was the woe the knight had in his mind
When they were escorted together to the marriage bed;
He tossed and turned restlessly to and fro.   1085
His old wife lay there, smiling all the while,
And said, "O my dear husband, goodness gracious!
Is this the way every knight behaves with his wife as you are with me?
Is this the custom in King Arthur's court?
Are all of his knights so disdainful?   1090
     "I am your own true love and your wife;
I am the one who saved your very life;
And truly, I have never yet done you any wrong,
Why do you treat me like this on our first night together?
You act as does a man who is out of his mind;   1095
What is my fault? For God's love tell it to me,
And it shall be amended, if it is in my power."

The knight's objections to marriage are two: the age and the ugliness of
the woman, and her lowly birth (she appears to be a peasant). What he must
learn is to recognize inner, moral beauty.

     Having maintained the discipline of the anonymous third person narrator
since digressing with the story of Midas' wife, the Wife of Bath re-enters the
narrative with an explanation of the lack of ceremony at the knight's
wedding (1073-1082). It appears to be an apology, or perhaps a self-
justification, but it is primarily neither. The truth is that the Wife cannot
resist stepping in to ram home just how miserable the knight is. As narrator,
she is gloating at the justice of his fate.

"Amended?" quod this knyght. "Allas, nay, nay!
It wol nat been amended nevere mo.
Thou art so loothly, and so oold also,   1100
And therto comen of so lough a kynde,
That litel wonder is thogh I walwe and wynde.
So wolde God myn herte wolde breste!"
     "Is this," quod she, "the cause of youre unreste?"
     "Ye, certeynly," quod he, "no wonder is."   1105
     "Now, sire," quod she, "I koude amende al this,
If that me liste, er it were dayes thre,
So wel ye myghte bere yow unto me.
     "But, for ye speken of swich gentillesse   1110
As is descended out of old richesse,
That therfore sholden ye be gentil men -
Swich arrogance is nat worth an hen!
Loke who that is moost vertuous alway,
Pryvee and apert, and moost entendeth ay
To do the gentil dedes that he kan;   1115
Taak hym for the grettest gentil man.
Crist wole we clayme of hym oure gentillesse,
Nat of oure eldres for hire old richesse.
For thogh they yeve us al hire heritage,
For which we clayme to been of heigh parage,   1120
Yet may they nat biquethe for no thing
To noon of us hir vertuous lyving,
That made hem 'gentil men' ycalled be,
And bad us folwen hem in swich degree."

It is the old woman who introduces the term "gentillesse" into the
discussion (1115). In doing so, she is fully aware of its ambiguity. The word
refers to the kinds of moral behavior and heightened sensibility which *should*
be exemplified by those born into the noble class. The problem comes, of
course, when men who are undoubtedly noble in the social sense do not *act*
morally. The debate recalls Chaucer's description of the Knight in *The
General Prologue*, "He was a verray, parfit gentil knight" (72). Prestwich
lists the chivalric ideals as: "*largesse*, or generosity; *courtoiseie*, or courtesy;
prouesse, or prowess; *loyauté*, or loyalty" (33), and whilst there is evidence
that Chaucer's Knight exemplifies, these qualities, there are other aspects of
the description that call his gentility into question.

"Remedied!" cried this knight. "Alas, no, no!
It will not ever be remedied, no!
You are so loathsome and so old,   1100
And moreover are so low-born,
That it is little wonder that I toss and turn
I wish to God my heart would burst!"
    "Is this," she asked, "the cause of your unhappiness?"
    "Yes, truly," said he, "and there is no wonder."   1105
    "Now, sir," said she, "I could put all this right,
If I had a mind to, and that within three days,
Provided you would act graciously towards me.
    "But since you introduce the topic of gentility   1110
Such as is inherited with family wealth,
And claim that because of it you should be regarded as a gentlemen,
I tell you straight that such arrogance is not worth a hen!
Find the person who is consistently the most virtuous,
In private or in public, and who always tries his hardest
To do whatever noble deeds he can,   1115
And take him as embodying what it means to be a gentleman.
Christ wills that we claim out gentility from Him,
Not from the wealth and social status of our ancestors.
Even though they pass on to us their heritage,
For which we claim to be nobly born,   1120
Yet they cannot by any means bequeath
To any of us their moral virtue,
Which is what made men call them 'gentlemen' in the first place,
And they bade us follow their example."

Here the knight has been stressing the social aspect of his gentility, but the old woman clearly has the better of the argument when she differentiates social from moral nobility. Cigman points out that "for the Wife and her audience the discourses on "gentilesse" and poverty within the *Tale* would not seem extraneous, because they regarded moral instruction as an integral part of the function of narrative literature" (12).

The old woman will support her own definition of gentility by citing an impressive range of textual authority. In this, the Wife makes her heroine the counterpart of Jankin who kept citing anti-feminist examples. Now it is payback time: the man must sit and listen to a female scholar showing an impressive depth of learning.

'Wel kan the wyse poete of Florence,   1125
That highte Dant, speken in this sentence.
Lo, in swich maner rym is Dantes tale:
"Ful selde upryseth by his branches smale
Prowesse of man, for God, of his goodnesse,
Wole that of hym we clayme oure gentilless."   1130
For of oure eldres may we no thyng clayme
But temporel thing, that man may hurte and mayme.
      "Eek every wight woot this as wel as I:
If gentillesse were planted naturelly
Unto a certeyn lynage doun the lyne,   1135
Pryvee and apert thanne wolde they nevere fyne
To doon of gentillesse the faire offyce;
They mighte do no vileynye or vyce.
      "Taak fyr and ber it in the derkeste hous
Bitwix this and the mount of Kaukasous,   1140
And lat men shette the dores and go thenne;
Yet wole the fyr as faire lye and brenne
As twenty thousand men mighte it biholde;
His offyce natureel ay wol it holde,
Up peril of my lyf, til that it dye."   1145

The old woman's argument starting at line 1133 is a paraphrase of *De Consolatione Philosophiae* by Boethius (c. 480–524 or 525 AD), a Christian philosopher of the early 6th century, rather than Dante who she first quotes. The argument is a very simple one: inanimate objects (like fire) get their essential properties from nature and, lacking free will, must exemplify those properties at all times. While a fire will burn whether anyone is watching it or not, a human being can behave differently in private than he/she does in public. Additionally, all fires have the same nature, but different individuals within the same family have different moral natures. In individual humans, moral nobility is a gift from God; God is its only source, and thus it is entirely independent of social status and wealth. The argument is unanswerable, and the old woman knows it.

Writing of the disquisition on "gentillesse," Cooper comments its "sheer length shifts the balance of the tale markedly from the story for its own sake towards story for the sake of a moral ... Nothing has led us to expect that either the Wife of Bath, with her social snobbery and her readiness to subordinate scriptural interpretation to her own sexual inclinations, or the Arthurian fairy shape-shifter, would be capable of the high idealism of 'Crist

'Well does that wise poet of Florence,   1125
Called Dante, know how to express himself on this subject.
What he says in the poem goes like this:
"Seldom upon the young branches of the family tree
Does moral worth mount up, and so it is ordained
That He who bestows it is its source."   1130
For from our fathers may we nothing claim
But worldly things that man can hurt and maim.
    "And everyone knows this as well as I:
If nobility were planted naturally
In the line of a particular family lineage,   1135
Then both in private and in public they would never cease
The ways of gentleness they had always followed
And could never fall to viciousness or vice.
    "Take fire and carry it into the darkest house
Between here and the Caucasus Mountains,   1140
And let men shut the doors and depart;
Nevertheless, the fire will blaze and burn as fairly
As if twenty thousand men were looking at it.
Its natural properties and function it continuously performs,
I swear it on my life, until it dies."   1145

wole we clayme of hym oure gentillesse' (1117). Least of all do we expect a
discourse on vice and virtue rather than men versus women … The Wife of
Bath has, I think, been left behind by this point" (Cooper 161-2). An even
more trenchant criticism is given by Wetherbee who argues that the lecture
"has no real function in the plot of the tale, and its irrelevance indicates the
limitation of the Wife of Bath's power to imagine a transformation of her
condition … Transformation does no more than fulfill a transparent fantasy
of sexual renewal … Success for women is still defined by marriage and
marriage is defined by male expectations" (82). My own view is that the
lecture on gentilesse *does* have a vital function in the plot, and that the whole
point is that we *should* all be talking about vice and virtue rather than about
male and female stereotypes. This argument is developed in the commentary.

    The reference to Dante is anachronistic on several levels. Firstly, the
story is set centuries before the birth of the poet Dante (c. 1265–1321), and
therefore the old hag could not possible cite him. Neither is there any
convincing way of explaining how the Wife of Bath would have become
familiar with Dante's work - she certainly didn't hear it in a sermon or from
Jankin's reading!

"Heere may ye se wel how that genterye
Is nat annexed to possessioun,
Sith folk ne doon hir operacioun
Alwey, as dooth the fyr, lo, in his kynde.
For, God it woot, men may wel often fynde   1150
A lordes sone do shame and vileynye;
And he that wole han prys of his gentrye,
For he was boren of a gentil hous
And hadde his eldres noble and vertuous,
And nyl hymselven do no gentil dedis,   1155
Ne folwen his gentil auncestre that deed is,
He nys nat gentil, be he duc or erl,
For vileyns synful dedes make a cherl.
    "For gentillesse nys but renomee
Of thyne auncestres, for hire heigh bountee,   1160
Which is a straunge thyng to thy persone.
Thy gentillesse cometh fro God allone.
Thanne comth oure verray gentillesse of grace.
It was no thing biquethe us with oure place."

This section largely repeats the argument of the previous section. The knight must understand this if he is to prove himself worthy of being saved: noble is as noble does. It is important to understand that the knight's education, his moral rehabilitation, is what the magic forces of fairy (in this case perfectly aligned with Christianity) have been contriving since his initial crime.

There is a great difference between the idealism of the old woman and the pragmatism of the Wife of Bath. In the Wife's battles with her husbands, material possessions were most definitely of primary importance to her. Only in fiction can she imagine the sort of values which would make mastery a concept foreign to any relationship, not just marriage.

"From this you can clearly see that true gentility
Is not connected to the wealth that a man may own,
Since folk do not behave consistently,
As the fire does according to its inherent nature.
For, God knows, that men may often discover   1150
A lord's son acting shamefully and villainously.
Therefore, he who prizes his gentility
Only because he was born of some old noble family,
With ancestors who were both highly placed in society and virtuous,
But yet will not himself do any noble deeds,   1155
Nor follow his deceased noble ancestor,
He is not gentle, be he a duke or an earl,
For villainous and sinful acts make a man a lout.

"Gentility is not just the reputation
That your ancestors gained for having shown charity and generosity,
If this is entirely alien to your character.   1161
Your gentility comes from God alone;
That, by the operation of grace, is the source of true nobility in man.
It was not inherited by us together with our rank and place in society."

Medieval bedchamber. Note the curtains surrounding the bed.
(*Illustrated History of Furniture, From the Earliest to the Present Time*
from 1893 by Litchfield, Frederick [1850-1930]. Wikimedia Commons.
Public domain.)

"Thenketh hou noble, as seith Valerius,   1165
Was thilke Tullius Hostillius,
That out of poverte roos to heigh noblesse.
Reedeth Senek, and redeth eek Boece;
Ther shul ye seen expres that it no drede is
That he is gentil that dooth gentil dedis.   1170
    "And therfore, leeve housbonde, I thus conclude:
Al were it that myne auncestres were rude,
Yet may the hye God, and so hope I,
Grante me grace to lyven vertuously.
Thanne am I gentil, whan that I biginne   1175
To lyven vertuously and weyve synne.
    "And ther as ye of poverte me repreeve,
The hye God, on whom that we bileeve,
In wilful poverte chese to lyve hys lyf,
And certes, every man, mayden, or wyf   1180
May understonde that Jhesus, hevene king,
Ne wolde nat chese a vicious lyving.
Glad poverte is an honest thing, certeyn;
This wole Senec and othere clerkes seyn.
Whoso that halt him payd of his poverte,   1185
I holde hym riche, al hadde he nat a sherte."

Cigman aptly comments, "Some readers may feel that the old woman is putting forward her supporting 'evidence' at the expense of the narrative, which has already been slowed to a standstill by the preceding philosophical discourse and which seems to be pushed aside entirely by this catalogue of Great Authors, incongruously offered in the nuptial bed!" (173).

A partial explanation can be found in the Wife of Bath's pride in displaying the depth of her reading and learning, but within the *Tale* there is a further justification. The whole point of the old woman's lecture is to challenge stereotypes, and a powerful medieval stereotype (one which justified treating women as second-class citizens) was the belief that they were not the intellectual equals of men. That is why girls did not go to school or university: education would have been wasted on them. Bombarded by citation after citation, the knight must acknowledge that, whatever else his wife may be, she is at least as well educated as is he.

"Consider how noble, as Valerius says,   1165
Was that same Tullius Hostilius,
Who rose out of poverty to high estate.
Read both Seneca and Boethius,
Where it is expressly stated that there is no doubt
That he is a gentleman who acts virtuously.   1170
     "And therefore, husband dear, I thus conclude:
Even though my ancestors were basely born,
Yet may the Lord God on high (so I trust)
Grant me the grace to live virtuously.
If I do, then I am noble from the moment I begin   1175
To live in virtue and to avoid sin.
     "And whereas you reproach me for my poverty,
The High God, in whom we all believe,
Voluntary chose to live His life in poverty,
And surely every man, or maid, or wife   1180
May understand that Jesus, Heaven's King,
Would never have chosen a blameworthy way of living.
Contented poverty is obviously a noble state
Which Seneca and other scholars maintain.
Whoever can be content with poverty,   1185
I regard him as rich, even though he has not got a shirt on his back."

"He that coveyteth is a povre wight,
For he wolde han that is nat in his might,
But he that noght hath, ne coveyteth have,
Is riche, although ye holde him but a knave.   1190
Verray poverte, it syngeth properly.
    "Juvenal seith of poverte myrily:
'The povre man, whan he goth by the weye,
Bifore the theves he may synge and pleye.'
    "Poverte is hateful good and, as I gesse,   1195
A ful greet bryngere out of bisynesse;
A greet amendere eek of sapience
To hym that taketh it in pacience.
Poverte is this, although it seme alenge,
Possessioun that no wight wol chalenge.   1200
Poverte ful ofte, whan a man is lowe,
Maketh his God and eek hymself to knowe.
Poverte a spectacle is, as thinketh me,
Thurgh which he may his verray freendes see.
And therfore, sire, syn that I noght yow greve,   1205
Of my poverte namoore ye me repreve."

The old woman's argument employs comic paradox: the poor are naturally happy because they never have to fear the loss of the little that they have, while the rich man lives in constant anxiety of thieves. The whole argument is summarized in the oxymoron, "Poverte is hateful good": men hate poverty because of the associations it has for them, but the state of poverty is actually a blessing.

Not for the last time, the old woman is trying to get the knight to 'think outside the box,' that is, to cast aside the assumptions about status which he has uncritically taken from society and think afresh for himself.

"He that covets wealth is a poor person,
For he wants what is beyond his power to achieve,
But he that has nothing and has no desires for more,
Is rich, although you regard him as only a poor man.   1190
True poverty is a naturally joyful state.
     "Juvenal wittily states of poverty:
'The poor man who walks along the highway
May stay calm and sing in the face of robbers.'
     "Poverty is a hated good, and, as I see it,   1195
It is a useful antidote to self-absorbing anxiety,
And a great encouragement of wisdom
In he who endures everything with due patience.
This is the true nature of poverty, though it seems to be misery,
A possession that no man will try to take away.   1201
Often poverty, when a man is low,
Makes him know both his God and even himself better.
Poverty is an eye-glass [lens], as it seems to me,
Through which a man may see who his true friends are.
Therefore, sir, since it is not harming you at all,   1205
Do not reproach me anymore for my poverty."

"Now, sire, of elde ye repreve me;
And certes, sire, thogh noon auctoritee
Were in no book, ye gentils of honour
Seyn that men sholde an oold wight doon favour   1210
And clepe him "fader," for youre gentillesse;
And auctours shal I fynden, as I gesse.
    "Now ther ye seye that I am foul and old,
Than drede you noght to been a cokewold;
For filthe and eelde, also moot I thee.   1215
Been grete wardeyns upon chastitee!
But nathelees, syn I knowe youre delyt,
I shal fulfille youre worldly appetyt.
    "Chese now," quod she, "oon of thise thynges tweye:
To han me foul and old til that I deye,   1220
And be to yow a trewe, humble wyf,
And nevere yow displese in al my lyf;
Or elles ye wol han me yong and fair,
And take youre aventure of the repair
That shal be to youre hous by cause of me,   1225
Or in som oother place, may wel be!
Now chese yourselven, wheither that yow lyketh."

The old woman's counter-argument against the knight's objections to her age (1208-9) begins almost exactly as goes the *Wife of Bath's Prologue* (1-2). On line 1211, she catches the knight in a logical trap: the very gentility to which he lays claim requires that he should show her respect because of her age and treat her kindly, not berate her about it. The old woman is running intellectual rings around the knight!

She appears to offer the knight two equally untenable options, but closer observation proves that this is not the case. Option one implies that sexual relations take place within the legal context of marriage and involve love and trust; option two implies that sex is an end in itself, a pleasure to be taken as and when the opportunity presents itself, without any sense of personal relationship and commitment. The idea of having a wife who is beautiful but promiscuous would probably have appeared rather attractive to the knight who raped the maiden by the river. For that man, sex was about exerting his male power over the woman, taking his pleasure where he chose, and completely ignoring the consequences. That the knight does not simply jump at the second option indicates how far he has come in his moral education.

132

"Now, sir, you have reproached me with my age;
And truly, sir, though there was no authority
In any book, men who are honored for their nobility
Say that you should treat an old person respectfully and kindly,
And call him 'father,' from your courtesy;   1211
And I know I could find authors to attest to this.
    "Now since you say that I am ugly and old,
Then you do not have to fear being made a cuckold;
For foul hideousness and age, I can assure you,   1215
Are mighty guardians over chastity!
But though I shall never be unfaithful, since I know what pleases you,
I'll satisfy your sexual appetites.
    "Choose, now," said she, "one of these two things:
To have me ugly and old until I die,   1220
And be to you a faithful and humble wife,
And never anger you in all my life;
Or else to have me young and beautiful
And take your chance with those men who will come
To your house because of me,   1225
Or perhaps arrange assignations with me in some other place.
Now you choose which you would prefer."

Leicester precisely defines what Alison means in both her *Prologue* and her *Tale* by having Jankin and the knight give up "mastrye" pointing out that in each case when the wife is given governance "she refrains from exercising it, and this suggests that it is primarily a tool for achieving feminine independence within marriage … making room for the possibility of love in the patriarchal world by giving women space to be responsible partners in a relationship" (Patterson 109). I can't improve on that!

This knyght avyseth hym and sore syketh,
But atte laste he seyde in this manere:
"My lady and my love, and wyf so deere,   1230
I put me in youre wyse governance;
Cheseth youreself which may be moost pleasance
And moost honour to yow and me also.
I do no fors the wheither of the two,
For as yow lyketh, it suffyseth me."   1235
        "Thanne have I gete of yow maistrie," quod she,
"Syn I may chese and governe as me lest?"
        "Ye, certes, wyf," quod he. "I holde it best."
        "Kis me," quod she. "We be no lenger wrothe,
For, by my trouthe, I wol be to yow bothe -   1240
This is to seyn, ye, bothe fair and good.
I prey to God that I moote sterven wood,
But I to yow be also good and trewe
As evere was wyf, syn that the world was newe.
And but I be to-morn as fair to seene   1245
As any lady, emperyce, or queene,
That is bitwixe the est and eke the west,
Dooth with my lyf and deth right as yow lest.
Cast up the curtyn, looke how that it is."

The knight must do four things to prove himself worthy: he must put control of his life entirely into the hands of his wife (as he took control entirely of the maiden he raped); he must accept the old woman as his wife without any reservations; he must love her; and he must prove the sincerity of all of the above by kissing this ugly old woman (an idea which he has earlier found repulsive).

The knight has won the right to a fresh start by totally subjugating his errant ego to the will of his wife. He addresses her as, "'My lady and my love, and wyf so deere'" (1230), thus establishing that, in terms of the tales of Courtly Love, he is her knight who he will serve in all things, that he loves her, and that he acknowledges her position as his legal wife. Recall that this is the man who married the old woman in secret and who when she laid claim to being "thy wyf... and eek thy love" (1066) replied, "My love? quod he, 'nay, my dampnacioun!'" (1067). He is now acknowledging everything which he formerly denied.

The dialogue between the knight and the old woman has taken place in their bed - a four poster with heavy side curtains. Thus, they have not

134

This knight thought it over carefully and sighed heavily, *huge contrast*

hyperbolic

But finally he spoke to this effect:

    "My lady and my love, and wife so dear,   1230

I put myself under your wise authority; *maybe he has learnt his lesson?*

Make choice yourself of which may be the more pleasing,

And which will bring to both you and I the most honor.

I care not which of these two things it is,

For whatever you decide will satisfy me."   1235

    "Then have you given to me the mastery," she said,

"Since I may choose and govern as I think fit?"

    "Yes, truly, wife," said he. "I hold that best."

    "Kiss me," said she. "We will no longer be angry with each other,

For, I vow, that to you I will be both;   1240

That is to say, yes, I shall be both morally good and beautiful.

I pray God that I shall go mad

If I am not to you as good and as true

As ever a wife was since the world was created.

And if, tomorrow at dawn, I am not as fair to look on   1245

As any lady, be she an empress or a queen

From the east to the west,

Do with my life and death just as you wish.

Throw back the curtain and see how things are now."

actually seen each other clearly since being ceremonially escorted to bed by the members of the court. It is now dawn, and the woman tells the knight (notice that she *tells* him, exerting the authority which he has given her) to pull up the hanging curtains and let in the light: symbolically it is the birth of a new day in each of their lives.

What the knight and his wife achieve is to reconcile two concepts that the *Prologue* presents as having been regarded for centuries as mutually exclusive: female beauty and female constancy. The authority of male writers (most of them, as the Wife of Bath points out, clerics) has traditionally associated sexual attractiveness with sin, for which reason men must ensure that women cover up their bodies in modest clothing and stay in the house. In the *Prologue*, the Wife of Bath describes her own rebellion against such attempts to take away her personhood. These took the form of defiance and promiscuity (that other company she had in youth about which it's better not to say too much!). In fiction, however, the Wife can envisage a third alternative in which the woman may be both fair and faithful.

And whan the knyght saugh verraily al this   1250
(That she so fair was, and so yong therto),
For joye he hente hire in his armes two,
His herte bathed in a bath of blisse.
A thousand tyme a-rewe he gan hire kisse,
And she obeyed him in every thing   1255
That myghte doon him plesance or lyking.

Having performed his quest and passed the trial of his faithfulness to his vow, the knight is considered to have expiated his former crimes, his misogyny and sexism, and made himself worthy of his reward. The modern reader, who has a more complex view of human psychology than did the fourteenth century reader, may be left a little unsatisfied.

The Wife of Bath has no such reservations. We can see her own enthusiasm for the resolution of her tale in the physical details of the young couple's love-making. The somewhat excessive nature of the serial kissing is plain enough, but there is a wonderfully coy reference to their experimental love-making in the lines, "And she obeyed hym in every thing / That myghte doon hym plesance or likyng" (1255-6). The narrator is clearly speaking from personal experience, and even more clearly identifies with her heroine.

The description of the two lovers enjoying a night of unrestrained passion is Alison's final reply to St. Jerome who in *Against Jovinian* writes, "A wise man ought to select his wife with careful judgment, not with the passion of love. Let a man govern his sexual impulses, and not rush headlong into intercourse. There is nothing worse than to love a wife as if she were a mistress. Men ... should behave to their wives as husbands not as lovers. In cases where marriage has grown out of lust, shameful to relate, men have tried to teach their wives chastity after having taken their chastity away. Marriages of that sort are quickly ended as soon as lust is satiated" (Author's version). The Wife will make it clear that the knight and his lady remained in love and married until their deaths.

The resolution is really existential: the knight wins everything he wants by giving up everything and by trusting implicitly in someone who gives him no grounds for trust at all; the woman who is not coerced into obedience is perfectly happy to tell her husband, "Dooth with my lyf and deth right as yow lest" (1248). Søren Kierkegaard would have understood completely! It is the knight's own misjudgments which have caused his suffering (to say nothing of the suffering of his victim), so he must give up his judgment and place his fate entirely in the hands of another person. Paradoxically, by doing so he proves himself worthy to take control not only of his own life but of his wife's also.

And when the knight saw the truth of all this,   1250
That she was so very beautiful, and also young,
For joy he clasped her in his two arms,
His heart bathed in a bath of utter bliss.
A thousand times, all in a row, he kissed her,
And she obeyed his wish in everything   1255
That might give him pleasure or delight.

In terms of the debate about sovereignty in marriage, the solution is both radical and very modern. Women want to be treated as equals. What they object to is being regarded *in law* as no more than the property of their husbands. Once a man gives up this 'official' discrimination, there is nothing for the two to fight about. Since the man is no longer ordering his wife about, she is, of course, perfectly happy to do just what he wants. She is, after all, madly in love with him and enjoys the physical aspect of their relationship just as much as (perhaps in Alison's case just a little more than) he does. It is a win-win situation!

The loathly lady becomes instantly beautiful.
(E.B.Bensell, 1893. Public domain.)

And thus they lyve, unto hir lyves ende
In parfit joye; and Jhesu Crist us sende
Housbondes meeke, yonge, and fressh abedde,
And grace t'overbyde hem that we wedde;   1260
And eek I praye Jhesu shorte hir lyves
That noght wol be governed by hir wyves;
And olde and angry nygardes of dispence,
God sende hem soone verray pestilence!

There is also a rather touching element of wish-fulfillment in the ending, for this fairy tale ends with a marriage of youth to youth, something which the Wife of Bath has never been able to achieve in her own life. However, the voice of the Wife makes a final intrusion into the narrative to pull the reader back to the real world. Cooper highlights the mismatch between the fairy tale ending and the Wife's concluding comment, "She may reassert the familiar theme of wifely domination in her final lines, but it is not exactly the moral expressed by the story" (Cooper 163). Similarly, Cigman points out that, while it was conventional to end a sermon (and the *Wife of Bath's Tale* is certainly an *exemplum,* a story told to illustrate an intellectual idea or a moral lesson) with a prayer, the content of the prayer "distinctly parodies the model" since it entreats God's aid towards the entirely worldly ends of providing women with compliant, generous, short-lived husbands and asks, in Jesus' name, for those husbands who are domineering and miserly to be punished by the plague (175). There is fantasy and then there is the real world!

And in this way they lived unto the end of their lives,
In perfect joy; and Jesus to us send
Meek husbands, and young ones, and fresh in bed,
And the good fortune to outlive those that we wed.   1260
And I pray Jesus to cut short the lives ← bitter
Of those who will not be governed by their wives,
And old and querulous misers in their spending,
And immediately send them a mortal plague!

fairy tale ending

Ended with a prayer
very sexual

Chapter 6: The Structure of the *Prologue* and *Tale*

There are twenty-three prologues in *The Canterbury Tale* of which the Wife of Bath's is much the longest allowing Chaucer to develop her history and character in more detail than those of any of the other pilgrims.

Structure of the *Prologue*

1-8 Summary biography of the Wife - her experience of marriage.

9-50 Defense of remarriage upon the death of one's spouse.

51-104 Defense of marriage itself.

105-153 Defense of sexual activity.

154-162 Defense of female dominance over the male within marriage.
>   **163-192** *First interruption:* Outburst of the Pardoner and the Wife's response.

193-502 History of the Wife's first four marriages:
>   **197-234** Account of her first three marriages - how she easily dominated her old doting husbands.
>   **235-451** The false accusations which she made against her husbands to put them in the wrong.
>   **452-502** Account of her fourth marriage - her husband's adultery.
>>   **455-480** *First digression:* The Wife describes herself in her youth and vigor.
>>   **481-502** How she made her fourth husband suffer for his unfaithfulness - his death.

503-524 Introduction to the account of her fifth marriage - Jankin's dominance of her.
>   **525-586** *Second digression:* Wife tells how she wooed Jankin.

587-599 Burial of husband number four - she falls in love with Jankin.
>   **600-626** *Third digression:* Wife describes her temperament - her combative nature and her enjoyment of sex.

627-687 The marriage to Jankin - their battles - his book of stories of the perfidy of women.
>   **688-710** *Fourth digression:* Wife's opinion on the bias of clerics against women - the clash of Venus and Mercury.

711-810 The climax of the *Prologue*: The stories against women that Jankin read one evening - the Wife ripping pages from his book - their fight.

811-827 Their eventual reconciliation - the Wife gains mastery - Jankin's death.

> **828-856** *Second interruption:* The argument between the Friar and the Summoner.

Structure of the *Tale*

857-881 **Exposition:** Description of the setting of the story - an England of Arthurian romance and fairy magic.

> **864-881** *First digression:* the Wife of Bath's bitterly satirical attack on Friars in contemporary England.

882-982 **Rising action:** The rape of the virgin maiden and the consequent quest for the answer to the Queen's question.

> **931-934** *Second digression:* The Wife's first opinion on an offered answer.
>
> **938-944** *Third digression:* The Wife's second opinion on an offered answer.
>
> **949-982** *Fourth digression:* The Wife's third opinion on an offered answer - leading to the story of Midas' wife.

983-1022 **Conflict:** The knight's meeting with the old woman and his promise in return for the answer to his quest.

1023-1218 **Falling action:** The marriage of the knight and the old woman and their going to bed - she delivers a lecture on gentility

> **1073-1082** *Fifth digression:* Explanation of the lack of description of the wedding celebrations.

1219-1264 **Resolution:** The knight gives mastery to his wife and receives his reward. They live happily ever after.

> **1258-1264** *Sixth digression*: The Wife of Bath's final prayer for young obedient and sexually satisfying husbands - and plenty of them.

Chapter 7: The Teller and the Tale

The Evidence of the Manuscripts

Chaucer never completed *The Canterbury Tales*, nor (so far as we can tell) were the tales that he did finish ever collected into a single volume during his lifetime. Therefore, we do not know the order in which Chaucer had decided that the tales should be told, or even if he had yet made that decision. None of Chaucer's original manuscripts survive; the text we use today derives from eighty-three different manuscripts, all handwritten (with the exception of William Caxton's edition of 1478), and all produced after Chaucer's death. These texts vary, partly as a result of copying errors and changes made by the original scribes and partly because they reflect different stages of Chaucer's revisions of the work. Rudd has this caution for the contemporary reader, "[W]e tend to assume that whichever modern text we are using, we are reading 'Chaucer', whereas in fact we are reading a carefully and skillfully reconstructed Chaucer, in which abbreviated word-forms have been expanded to make them comprehensible to us and modern punctuation has been brought in" (100).

There is some evidence that Chaucer did not originally intend the tale of the knight and the loathly lady to be told by the Wife of Bath. Some manuscripts of *The Man of Law's Tale* contain an epilogue in which an anonymous pilgrim vows:

> My handsome body shall tell a tale,
> And I shall clink you so merry a bell,
> That I shall liven up the whole company.
> But it will not be about philosophy,
> Nor legal cases, nor abstruse lawyers' terms.
> (*The Man of Law's Epilogue* 1185-9 Author's modernization)

This indicates that, at that time, Chaucer envisaged the Wife of Bath telling the story which the Shipman now tells and had not yet decided who would tell the story of the knight and the old hag. Further evidence that this was the author's original intention is found in the fact that *The Shipman's Tale* was originally meant to have a female narrator. Of course, the only women on the pilgrimage to Canterbury are the Wife of Bath, the Prioress, and the Second Nun, but, since *The Shipman's Tale* is a bawdy fabliau, one can only conceive of the Wife of Bath telling it.

The Shipman's Tale tells of a merchant's wife young, vivacious wife who, for one hundred franks, sells a night of sex to her husband's best friend, John the Monk. He then attempts to trick her out of the money he has given her. The young wife is triumphant in the end, however, since she contrives to spend the money, to hide her infidelity from her husband, and to convince him to accept repayment of the money he has lost in the form of plenty of sex with her. Such a story appears to have little connection with the character of the Shipman, although it certainly lives up to his promise:

> 'And I shall clink you so merry a bell,
> That I shall wake up everyone in this company.
> But it shall not be of philosophy,
> Nor legal cases, nor elaborate terms of law.
> There is but little Latin in my mouth!'
> (1186-1190 Author's modernization)

Other than this rather perfunctory effort to make the tale fit the teller, the best that critics have come up with is that the Shipman in *The General Prologue* is depicted as a deceiving thief, like John the Monk in the tale, and that shipmen and merchants were, in the fourteenth century, noted for their mutual animosity which may explain why the merchant is the butt of the tale's satire. This is pretty superficial. On the other hand, the anti-clericalism of the tale, the theme of a young wife's love of material possessions, her cunning unfaithfulness, and the emphasis on sex both within and outside of marriage certainly fit with the character of the Wife as it develops in her *Prologue*.

The opening of *The Shipman's Tale*, which describes a Merchant in St. Denis who is married to a young, beautiful, and lively woman whose sociability is expensive, makes it clear that the narrator is on the side of women. The use of pronouns in the assertion that the husband must pay such costs establishes that the narrator is a woman:

The sely husband algate he must pay,	The helpless husband must always pay,
He must *us* clothe and he must us array	He must buy *us* clothes and adornments
All for his owen worship richely:	for the sake of his reputation:
In which array *we* dance jollily.	In which finery *we* dance joyfully.
And if that he may not, paraventure,	And if it happens that he cannot pay,
Or elles list not such dispence endure,	Or does not wish to spend so much,
But thinketh it is wasted and y-lost,	Thinking it is just loss or wasteful,
Then must another paye for *our* cost,	Then another man must give *us* money,
Or lend *us* gold, and that is perilous.	Or lend *us* gold, and that has dangers.

(10-19 Author's modernization, emphasis added)

The Wife of Bath would certainly agree with this picture of marital relationship, or at least the mercenary and combative side of her character would. What *The Shipman's Tale* fails to reflect, however, is the romantic idealism which hides behind this mercenary and combative side and becomes evident in her brief, but touching, picture of her life with Jankin after they have reached their understanding and of her continuing love for him after his death. Evidently, this is why Chaucer changed his original intention about which tale Alison would tell.

The Wife of Bath and Her Tale

Given what we surmise about Chaucer's reasons for the allocation the tale of the knight and the old hag to the Wife of Bath, the obvious question is: To what extent they are a good fit for each other? On this point critical opinion is divided. Rossignol writes:

> [The Wife of Bath] is the closest Chaucer came to creating a fully realized dramatic persona ... [The tale] seems by its subject matter to perfectly correspond to the concerns and preoccupations of its teller. (297-300)

In contrast, Cigman finds that her story "very different in mood and tone from her *Prologue*" (9). William neatly reconciles the two positions when he comments, "it seems to me that the Wife's tale and prologue can be treated as one lengthy monologue, and it is the voice we attribute *that* monologue too which proves impossible to precisely define" (GradeSaver, emphasis in original).

The most obvious way in which Chaucer adapts the *Tale* to Alison is in the six digressions which follow a narrative pattern set in the *Prologue* and in which her vocabulary and speech patters can be readily identified. Nor are these digressions simply arbitrary additions, for as Cigman rightly asserts, "The Wife's direct involvement in her *Tale* is not *merely* the result of her desire to assert herself: her personal interpolations are meant to endorse the *truth* of what she is relating" (11). However, one feature of the tale that she tells which does not appear appropriate to the Wife is its genre. As Cooper points out, "The Wife of Bath is the "only character to tell a romance who has no claim to gentil status or to connections at court" (157). Cooper defends the choice of an aristocratic genre by relating it to Alison's assertion of her social superiority over the other wives of her parish, and by arguing that, "By giving her a romance, Chaucer adds another side to her character: she is an incurable romantic ... The tale may be overtly about women's love of sovereignty. But it ends with marital - and especially sexual - bliss" (156).

Other aspects of tale may be seen as appropriate to a woman in her mid-forties who is painfully aware of the beauty and liveliness which the years have stolen from her. Thus, the narrator chooses to give no description of the ugliness of the old hag (perhaps because it would hit too close to home). In addition, the story ends with the transformation of an old crone into the vivacious young woman Alison once was herself, married to a handsome and virile young man as she also once was. On this level the tale functions as sheer wish fulfillment.

144

The Wife effectively tells not one but two tales: one a naturalistic history of her marriages and the other a romantic Breton lay set in the age of Camelot. Ultimately, it is in the thematic parallels between *Prologue* and *Tale* that Chaucer convinces us that only the Wife of Bath could tell this tale, for the tale of the knight exactly parallels the history of Jankin and of men in general as it is described in the *Prologue*. In order to make this, Chaucer has to adapt the folk tale upon which the narrative is based. In no other extant version of the Loathly Lady story is the plot set in motion by a rape. Chaucer's innovation is masterly because rape is the logical extension of Jankin's determination to establish male mastery over what he regards as his morally and intellectually inferior wife. Similarly, in no other version of the tale is the knight asked to choose between beauty and faithfulness. In other extant versions, the choice is between having the wife young and beautiful during the day or during the night. The question in the Wife's tale is more realistic in the sense that it rests upon the same suspicion of female beauty to which Alison referred in her *Prologue* when putting accusations into the mouths of her husbands:

> ... if that she be fair, thou verray knave,
> Thou seyst that every holour will hire have;
> She may no while in chastitee abyde,
> That is assailled upon ech a side! (253-6)

It is this fear which led Alison's fourth and fifth husbands to seek to stop her gadding around and about which Jankin has been reading in his book: men (particularly clerics) believe that, given their inherent sinfulness derived from Eve, the only guarantee of faithfulness in a woman is age and ugliness.

The point of each of Alison's two narratives is to assert not only that women can be faithful and dutiful, but also that a marriage can be a union of equals. As Cigman points out, "Like the Wife's fifth husband, [the knight] achieves the gratification of all his wishes by first substituting his wife's will for his own" (13-4). There is something even more fundamental behind this, however, for neither man would have relinquished sovereignty had they not themselves learned to respect women - the temperamental transformation of Alison and the physical and temperamental transformation of the Loathly Lady are contingent upon a complete change in the outlook of their husbands. In Jankin's case, the turning point is his horror at having struck his wife so violently that he really believes for a few moments that he has killed her, and in the knight it is his acceptance of his wife's definition of "gentilesse." Thus, the ultimate similarity between the *Prologue* and the *Tale* is that neither is really about "sovereignty over the husband, but rather a pledge of mutual love and service that led to this satisfying relationship" (Rossignol 301).

A Marriage Debate

It was the critic Kittredge, writing in 1914, who advanced the theory that in telling her *Prologue* and *Tale* the Wife of Bath sets off a chain-reaction which impacts the tales that follow, particularly those of the Clerk, Merchant, and Franklin, all of which deal to some degree with the subject of where authority lies in marriage and how it should be exercised. Most immediately, Alison's narratives spark what appears to be a long-standing animosity between the Friar and the Summoner resulting in a pair of tales each designed to discredit the other in which marriage plays a peripheral role. It is with the Clerk's tale that Kittredge identifies the first considered reply to Alison who had specifically blamed clerks for their misogynistic views.

The Clerk tells the story of Walter, a marquis, who marries a poor peasant girl, Griselda, and then tests her loyalty in a number of cruel ways. Griselda, however, remains subservient and obedient, and eventually, having passed every test, the two live happily. Having concluded his tale, the Clerk states with bitter irony:

> But one word, lords, listen before I conclude:
> It would be very difficult nowadays to find,
> Even in a whole town, two or three Griseldas;
> For if they were put to such tests,
> The gold of them has now been so badly debased
> With brass, that though the coin is fair to see,
> It would more easily break in two than bend.
> For which at this point, for the love of the Wife of Bath
> (Whose life and all her sect may God maintain
> In high mastery, for to do otherwise would be a pity)
> I will, with lusty heart, fresh and young
> Recite a song that will, I believe, make you all happy.
> (1163-74 Author's modernization)

It is clear that, behind the superficial courtesy, this is a lament that the days of patient wives are passed and an attack on the Wife of Bath and all of her heretical sect. Worse still, the Clerk concludes with a song in which, with biting satire, he appears to encourage wives to follow the advice of the Wife of Bath and dominate their husbands:

> O noble wives, full of great wisdom,
> Let no humility nail down your tongue,
> Nor let any clerk have cause or inspiration
> To write about you a story of such wonder
> As that of patient and kind Griselda ...
> (1183-7 Author's modernization)

146

The Clerk has used all of his considerable rhetorical skill to attack Alison.

The Clerk's story of patient Griselda strikes a chord with the Merchant because his own wife is nothing like Griselda, so much so that he wishes profoundly that he had never allowed himself to be trapped into marriage:

> I have a wife, the worst that could be,
> For though the devil himself were married to her,
> She would outmatch him, I dare well swear.
> Why should I tell you in great detail
> Of her proud malice? She is a shrew in every way.
> There is a long and large difference
> Between Griselda's great patience
> And the extreme cruelty of my wife ...
> (1218-25 Author's modernization)

The Merchant tells us that he has been married only two months! Sensing a good story, the Host urges him to speak of the "art" which women use to make their husbands miserable, and the Merchant readily agrees though he states that he will make his point in a story rather than by dwelling on his own situation. The Merchant tells of January, a sixty-year-old knight from Pavia, who marries the beautiful May, who is just twenty. Unsurprisingly, May falls for a handsome young squire, Damyan, with whom she manages to have sex right before her husband's eyes and yet get away with it by convincing him that he is seeing things. She even hints to him that he may suffer similar delusions in the future!

The Merchant's story results in an outburst from the Host:

> Lo, what tricks and craftiness
> Is in women! For always they are as busy as bees
> To deceive us simple men,
> From the truth they will always turn away ...
> (2421-4 Author's modernization)

The Host is drawn into a complaint about his own wife's shrewish behavior, but cuts himself short saying that someone in the group (Kittredge confidently identifies the Wife of Bath) may repeat his complaints to his wife on their return to London.

This litany of strife in marriage is concluded by the Franklin whose story illustrates that love is indeed compatible with marriage. Arveragus, a French knight, marries Dorigen for love and they agree that theirs will be a union of equals, although for the sake of appearances Arveragus will seem to take the decisions in public. Whilst Arveragus is away in England, Dorigen is tricked by Aurelius into agreeing to sleep with him. Upon his return, Dorigen explains her predicament to Arveragus who tells her that she must stand by her word and assures her that he will continue to love her. The tale has a happy ending, however, since the evident love of Arveragus and Dorigen prompts Aurelius to withdraw his claim on Dorigen.

To Kittredge, the Franklin provides the finishing act to the Marriage Group of tales, but it is fair to say that more critical ink has been spent on the concept of the Marriage Debate than on any other single aspect of *The Canterbury Tales*. The reader should regard this sketch as no more than an introduction.

Chapter 8: Three Tales of the Loathly Lady

No source for Chaucer's *The Wife of Bath's Tale* can be identified; it is probably based on a well-known folk tale. Three other works in English also appear to draw on the same folk tale: John Gower's *Tale of Florent* from *Confessio Amantis* (*The Lover's Confession*, c. 1386-90), the anonymous *The Weddynge of Sir Gawen and Dame Ragnell*, and *The Marriage of Sir Gawaine*. Of these, only the *Tale of Florent* is strictly contemporary with Chaucer, *The Weddynge of Sir Gawen and Dame Ragnell* being fifteenth century, and *The Marriage of Sir Gawaine* a ballad of uncertain date first collected in the Percy Folio in the seventeenth century.

John Gower's *Tale of Florent*

Summary:

Florent, nephew to the emperor and a knight of great fame for his chivalry, is captured during a skirmish on the border in which he kills Branchus, the son of his captor. The father desires revenge for the death of his son, but, aware of Florent's reputation and his imperial connections, he cannot simply execute him. The grandmother of Branchus suggests a stratagem which will allow Florent to be killed without any blame attaching to them: she will get him to agree that his life will be forfeit if he cannot answer the question, 'What do all women most desire?'

Florent agrees to the terms of the agreement and is set free to wander. He returns to the emperor's court where all the wise men fail to come up with an answer. Leaving to meet his doom, Florent reminds his uncle that he vowed to honor the agreement to answer the question or die, and that therefore no revenge should be taken for his death.

In a wood, he encounters a loathly old woman who appears to know his predicament. She offers him the benefit of her advice, in return for which he agrees that she shall have whatever she asks for. The old woman asks for his hand in marriage, but the knight tries to dissuade her. Nothing availing, it occurs to Florent that without the answer he is going to be put to death, that the woman is old and will soon die, and that, until then, he can put her on an island to live in secret, so he agrees to her terms, and she tells him that all women want to be sovereign of a man's love.

Florent returns to his captors and successfully answers the question before Branchus' family, much to their horror. He returns to the loathly lady and, despite his revulsion, knows that as a knight he must marry her according to his promise. Traveling by night, he takes her secretly to his castle where he tells only his most trusted people about his situation. The old woman is bathed and dressed in finery, though nothing can mask her ugliness.

The two are married in the dark of night, and declaring herself to be happy, the old woman takes Florent to bed where she insists upon him making love to her. The bed chamber being full of light, Florent turns away so as not to have to look at his bride, but she eventually gets him to turn toward her. When he does, he sees a beautiful woman, eighteen years of age. She tells him that he must choose whether to have her beautiful during the day or during the night, for he may not have both.

Florent admits that he simply cannot choose and puts the decision entirely into his wife's hands. By acknowledging her sovereignty, his wife tells him, he has freed her from her cursed fate, and his reward is that she will be beautiful both day and night. She identifies herself as the daughter of the King of Sicily, placed under a curse of ugliness by her hateful stepmother which could only be broken by winning sovereignty from a knight of high repute. The two live happily ever after. Clergy later interpret the story to show how obedience leads to true love rather than mere lust.

The Tales of Gower and Chaucer Compared

Apart from the obvious similarity of the basic plot, the most important parallel between the two tales is the centrality of the theme of mastery in marriage. In answer to the question, 'What thing is it that women most desire?' the old hag in Gower introduces the concept of 'sovereignty':

'... thou schalt seie, upon this molde...	'... you shall say that in this world
That alle wommen lievest wolde	What all women would most desire
Be soverein of mannes love:	Is to be sovereign of man's love:
For what womman is so above,	For such a woman is superior to the rest,
Sche hath, as who seith, al hire wille;	Because she has everything she wants;
And elles may sche noght fulfille	Otherwise, she could not get
What thing hir were lievest have.'	The thing she most wants to have.'

(1607-1612 Clarendon Press, Author's modernization, emphasis added)

Similarly, when Florent gives his wife the power to answer the question which she poses on their wedding night, he concedes 'mastery':

'I not what ansuere I schal give:	'I know not what answer I should give:
Bot evere whil that I may live,	But as long as I live

I wol that ye be my maistresse,	I want you to be my ruler,
For I can noght miselve gesse	For I cannot myself determine
Which is the beste unto my chois.	Which one is the better choice.
Thus grante I yow myn hole vois,	Thus I grant you my whole voice:
Ches for ous bothen, I you preie;	Choose for us both, I pray you;
And what as evere that ye seie,	And whatever you decide,
Riht as ye wole so wol I.'	Just as you will, so will I.'

(1822-1830 Clarendon Press, Author's modernization, emphasis added)

By this speech, as the lady remarks, Florent has made her "sovereign" (1833) and so released her from the curse of ugliness.

The problem with Gower's tale is that it provides no meaningful context for the theme of sovereignty/mastery. Although *Confessio Amantis* has a frame story (being the confessions of Amans, or the Lover, to Venus), the tale has no individualized narrator whose life and *Prologue* exemplify its theme, and even within the narrative itself sovereignty/mastery appears to be attached to nothing. The knight commits no crime; he falls into the power of the grandmother (the equivalent of Chaucer's Queen) by the misfortunes of battle. Therefore, the question set has nothing to do with the knight's education and rehabilitation: it is simply a question which the grandmother believes he will never be able to answer. Similarly, the loathly lady has been condemned to ugliness by her wicked stepmother for no particular reason, and the condition that she cannot regain her youth and beauty until she "hadde wonne / The love and sovereineté / Of what knyht that in his degree / Alle othre passeth of good name" (1845-8) appears to be entirely arbitrary, no reason for it being given. Finally, the choice which the lady offers Florent also lacks any connection with the theme of sovereignty/mastery, its only point being (once again) that it is a very difficult choice to make.

In contrast, Chaucer not only relates the tale thematically with the Wife's *Prologue*, but also ensures that the theme of sovereignty/mastery is central to everything in the narrative itself. Thus, the knight's rape of the maiden, which is found in none of the other British versions, is the ultimate expression of the view that males should have authority over females, and as such it is the equivalent to the attempts of the Wife's fourth and fifth husbands to restrict her freedom. Whilst Gower's antagonist-lovers are named and even given a brief, individualizing biography, Chaucer's knight and loathly lady are anonymous; they "are never named: they remain embodiments of a male and female principle ... paradigms in the battle between the sexes" (Cooper 158). The Queen's choice of question fits the knight's crime, for he must learn to see the world through other than male eyes. The loathly lady is a fairy spirit (no victim she!) who has the magical power not only to transform herself but also to wipe away the sin of the knight's crime. This is why Chaucer changes the question that the knight must answer from a meaningless choice between night and day to a choice between "virtue and beauty - an issue much more in keeping with ... the Wife's *Prologue*" (Cooper 158). The knight's giving the choice to the wife, allows Chaucer to reconcile the worlds of the flesh and of the spirit - the very debate which pervades the *Prologue*. Clerics have associated female beauty with lust and the sins of the flesh and blamed women for tempting men from the path to heaven, but the young wife is able to show that the two are compatible: a beautiful wife may be both pure and dutiful. Additionally, the resolution of their story proves that, within marriage, a loving couple may enjoy all the glorious sex they want without the least taint of sin.

There are, of course, other important differences between the two tales. Thus whilst Chaucer deals with the loathly lady's appearance in one line, "A fouler wight ther may no man devyse" (999), leaving the rest to the reader's imagination, Gower goes into minute detail in describing her:

This olde wyht him hath awaited	The old woman had waited for him
In place wher as he hire lefte:	In the place where he had left her.
Florent his wofull heved uplefte	Florent raised up his woeful head,
And syh this vecke wher sche sat,	And saw this hag where she sat;
Which was the lothlieste what	She was the loathliest crone
That evere man caste on his yhe:	That man ever cast an eye upon:
Hire Nase bass, hire browes hyhe,	Her nose hung low, her brows arched high,
Hire yhen smale and depe set,	Her eyes were small and deep set;
Hire chekes ben with teres wet,	With tears her cheeks were always wet,
And rivelen as an emty skyn	And wrinkled as an empty wine skin,
Hangende doun unto the chin,	Hanging in folds down on her chin.
Hire Lippes schrunken ben for age,	Her lips were shrunk with age;
Ther was no grace in the visage,	Her face had not a single saving grace;
Hir front was nargh, hir lockes hore,	Her forehead was narrow, her hair grey,
Sche loketh forth as doth a More,	She glowered like a Blackamoor.
Hire Necke is schort, hir schuldres courbe,	Her neck is short, her shoulders rounded:
That myhte a mannes lust destourbe,	All manly lust she could deflate;
Hire body gret and nothing smal,	Her form was gross and not petite,
And schortly to descrive hire al,	And briefly to complete the description,
Sche hath no lith withoute a lak;	She had no part without defect;
Bot lich unto the wollesak	But, like a tattered wool sack,
Sche proferth hire unto this knyht,	She offered herself to this knight,
And bad him, as he hath behyht	And bade him, since he'd seen
So as sche hath ben his warant,	That she had saved his life,
That he hire holde covenant,	He must hold to the agreement,
And be the bridel sche him seseth.	And by the horse's bridle seized him.

(1672-1697 Clarendon Press, Author's modernization)

The reader will decide on which he/she prefers. (Personally, I think the Gower passage is pretty good.) The reason that Chaucer is so brief is that his story, unlike that of Gower, uses incident to explore ideas: the Wife of Bath cannot wait to get onto the message of her exemplum.

In two instances, Chaucer shows himself superior to Gower in simple narrative skill. Firstly, whilst the hag in Gower's tale presents her demand for marriage *before* he agrees to receive the answer from her, in Chaucer she makes him agree only to fulfill her first wish. It is not until after he has successfully answered the Queen's question, and is feeling pretty relieved, that she springs her trap. Secondly, whilst Gower's hag tells the knight (and the reader) immediately he agrees to her terms that all women want sovereignty in love (1608-10), Chaucer has her whisper the secret to the knight, "Thor owned she a pistel in his ere" (1021), leaving the reader in suspense until the climax of the story before the Queen's court.

Finally, in Chaucer the transformation of the old crone into a beauty only occurs after the knight has given her mastery (1228-54). This is effective because the knight has no idea that he will get a reward for giving the correct response, and neither does the reader. In contrast, Florent turns to see a beautiful young woman beside him and only then does she confront him with the day/night question:

The chambre was al full of lyht,	The chamber was all filled with light,
The courtins were of cendal thinne	The curtains were of thin cendal cloth;
This newe bryd which lay withinne,	This new bride, who lay there within,
Thogh it be noght with his acord,	Though it was not with his consent,
In armes sche beclipte hire lord,	In her arms she embraced her lord,
And preide, as he was torned fro,	And prayed, since he was turned away,
He wolde him torne ayeinward tho;	He'd turn around to where she lay,
'For now,' sche seith, we ben bothe on.'	'For now,' she said, 'we're both one.'
And he lay stille as eny ston,	And he lay as still as any stone,
Bot evere in on sche spak and preide,	But she spoke steadfastly and prayed
And bad him thenke on that he seide,	And bade him think about his vows
Whan that he tok hire be the hond.	When he had married her.
He herde and understod the bond,	He heard and understood the obligation,
How he was set to his penance,	How he must pay his penance.
And as it were a man in trance	Then, like a man in a trance,
He torneth him al sodeinly,	He turned around quite suddenly,
And syh a lady lay him by	And saw a lady by his side
Of eyhtetiene wynter age,	Just eighteen winters old,
Which was the faireste of visage	With the fairest face that
That evere in al this world he syh:	His eyes had ever seen in this world;
And as he wolde have take hire nyh,	And as he drew her near,
Sche put hire hand and be his leve	She raised her hand and, by his leave,
Besoghte him that he wolde leve,	Beseeched that he would desist.
And seith that for to wynne or lese	And said that to either win or lose,
He mot on of tuo thinges chese,	He must choose between two things:
Wher he wol have hire such on nyht,	Whether to have her thus at night,

| Or elles upon daies lyht, | Or else during the day's light. |
| For he schal noght have bothe tuo. | For he may not have both the two. |

(1786-1813 Clarendon Press, Author's modernization)

Gower does not come close either to the dramatic effect which Chaucer achieves or to showing the transformation of the old hag as being central to the theme of the tale.

Weddynge of Sir Gawen and Dame Ragnell (**Anonymous**)

Summary:

Hunting in Inglewood, King Arthur kills a fine deer, but in doing so becomes separated from his knights. He is ambushed by Sir Gromer Somer who accuses Arthur of having given his land illegally to Sir Gawain. Arthur wins his life only by agreeing to return alone in one year with the answer to the question: 'What do women love best?'

Arthur returns to Carlisle and tells only Gawain about the challenge. Gawain suggests that the two ride separately about the country collecting and writing answers in a book. Eleven months later, Arthur returns to Inglewood where he encounters an ugly old woman, Dame Ragnell, who promises to give him the answer on condition that he marries her to Sir Gawain. Arthur refuses to agree without asking Gawain, so he returns to Carlisle. Gawain agrees out of love and duty for the King who returns to Dame Ragnell with his word, and she tells him that all women desire sovereignty.

When the year is up, Arthur returns to Sir Gromer. He goes through all of the answers he has collected, but they are rejected. Finally, Arthur gives Dame Ragnell's answer. The furious Sir Gromer reveals that the old woman is his sister.

Ragnell returns to Carlisle with Arthur who tries to have the wedding in secret, but she insists on a lavish, public marriage before the whole court. She is dressed even more finely that Queen Guinevere, and after the ceremony she eats ravenously just about everything at the splendid wedding banquet.

Gawain and Ragnell retire to bed, and Ragnell insists that her husband make love to her as is expected. He turns towards her to find his wife transformed into the most beautiful woman he has ever seen. She offers him a choice: she can be beautiful either at night or during the day. Gawain cannot decide, and gives his wife the authority to make the decision. Delighted, she tells him that he has broken a curse placed on her by her stepmother: now that the foremost knight in England has given her sovereignty, she can be beautiful all the time. The couple stays awake all night making love.

When Arthur goes to Gawain's bedchamber the next morning, the knight shows him his beautiful wife. The delighted King rejoices and tells the court about Sir Gromer's challenge; Gawain tells how his wife came to be cursed; and Ragnell tells how Gawain removed the curse by giving her sovereignty. Ragnell asks Arthur to correct the injustice originally done to her brother, Sir Gromer Somer. Ragnell and Gawain live in perfect harmony and happiness and have a son, Gyngolyn, who eventually joins the Round Table. However, their happiness is brief, for after only five years Ragnell dies, and though Gawain marries often in his life, he never loves another as he did Ragnell. The poem concludes with a prayer that its author be released from prison

The Wedding of Gawain and *The Wife of Bath's Tale* Compared:

The above summary indicates that *The Weddynge of Sir Gawen and Dame Ragnell* has much more in common with John Gower's *Tale of Florent* than it does with *The Wife of Bath's Tale*. There is no frame story and therefore no narrator to whom the themes of the story can be related. Once again, within the narrative itself, there is no meaningful context for the theme of sovereignty/mastery. The quest does begin with an injustice of sorts, but it is Arthur's 'crime' not Gawain's, and the question posed is even more arbitrary than in Gower's tale since it is asked by a man.

Only two significant points really differentiate the tale of Gawain from that of Florent. Firstly, whilst Florent manages to marry his loathly lady secretly in his own castle, Gawain's marriage to Ragnell takes place with full pomp at court and his wife makes a real exhibition of herself by eating voraciously at the wedding feast:

She ette thre capons, and also curlues thre,
And greatt bake metes she ete up, perdé.
Al men therof had mervaylle.
Ther was no mete cam her before
Butt she ete itt up, lesse and more…
(610-4 Thomas Hahn, Author's modernization)

She ate three capons and three curlews.
And a lot of roast meat, by God.
Everyone was astonished at it.
No food was put before her
But she ate it up, every bit…

Secondly, the ending avoids the fairy tale chiché that they both lived happily ever after. Neither point, however, has any relationship with Chaucer's tale.

Like Gower, the anonymous poet describes the loathly lady at length:

Her face was red, her nose snotyd withalle,
Her mowithe wyde, her tethe yalowe
overe alle,
With bleryd eyen gretter then a balle.
Her mowithe was nott to lak:
Her tethe hyng overe her lyppes,
Her chekys syde as wemens hippes.
A lute she bare upon her bak;
Her nek long and therto greatt;
Her here cloteryd on an hepe;
In the sholders she was a yard brode.
Hangyng pappys to be an hors lode,
And lyke a barelle she was made.
And to reherse the fowlnesse of that Lady,
Ther is no tung may telle, securly;
Of lothynesse inowghe she had.

Her face was red, her nose snotty too,
Her mouth wide and her teeth all
yellow,
With bleared eyes bigger than a ball.
Her mouth wasn't too small either:
Her teeth protruded over her lips,
Her cheeks as broad as women's hips.
She had a hump upon her back;
Her neck was long and very thick;
Her hair was dirty and all in a heap;
She was a yard broad in the shoulders.
Her breasts needed a horse to carry,
And she was shaped like a barrel.
And to summarize the lady's ugliness
Surely, it was beyond description;
Of loathliness she had enough and to
spare.

(231-45 Thomas Hahn, Author's modernization)

Gawain responds more generously than does Florent to his wife's insistence that he should make love to her, and so the tale is even more a demonstration of the inherent nobility and courtesy of the hero who may be said to earn his wife's beauty by his conduct. In neither the case of Florent nor of Gawain is there anything that we might call character development.

After the loathly lady's transition, however, Gawain is posed the day or night question exactly as in the Florent tale:

'A, Sir Gawen, syn I have you wed,
Shewe me your cortesy in bed;
With ryghte itt may nott be denyed.
Iwyse, Sir Gawen,' that Lady sayd,
'And I were fayre ye wold do anoder brayd
Butt of wedlok ye take no hed.
Yett for Arthours sake kysse me att the leste;
I pray you do this att my request.

'Ah, Sir Gawain, since I am your wife,
Do your duty to me in bed;
You cannot rightfully refuse.
Certainly, Sir Gawain,' the Lady said
'If I were fair you'd act differently
Unless you have no regard for marriage.
But, for Arthur's sake, at least kiss me;
I beg you, do this at my request.

156

Lett se howe ye can spede.'	Let's see how you perform.'
Sir Gawen sayd, 'I wolle do more	Sir Gawain said, 'I shall do more
Then for to kysse, and God before!'	Than just kiss you, before God!'
He turnyd hym her untille.	He turned towards her until
He sawe her the fayrest creature	He saw the most beautiful woman
That evere he sawe, withoute mesure.	He'd ever set eyes on, beyond compare.
She sayd, 'Whatt is your wylle?'	She said, 'What is your will?'
'A, Jhesu!' he sayd; 'Whate ar ye?	'Ah, Jesus!' he said. 'Who are you?'
'Sir, I am your wyf, securly.	'Sir, certainly I am your wife.
Why ar ye so unkynde?'	Why are you so cruel?'
'A, Lady, I am to blame.	'Ah, Lady, I am to blame.
I cry you mercy, my fayre madame -	I ask your forgiveness, lady -
Itt was nott in my mynde.	I was just not thinking.
A Lady ye ar fayre in my syghte,	Ah Lady, you are beautiful to see,
And today ye were the foulyst wyghte	Yet today you were the foulest person
That evere I sawe with mine ie.	That I ever set eyes upon.
Wele is me, my Lady, I have you thus'	I am lucky to have you like this.'
And brasyd her in his armys and gan her kysse	And he embraced her and began to kiss her
And made greatt joye, sycurly.	And was certainly very happy.
'Syr,' she sayd, 'thus shalle ye me have:	'Sir,' she said, 'you will have me like this:
Chese of the one, so God me save,	Choose one, so God save my soul,
My beawty wolle nott hold -	My beauty will not stay put:
Wheder ye wolle have me fayre on nyghtes	Whether you will have me fair at night
And as foulle on days to alle men sightes,	And as ugly in the day as any man saw,
Or els to have me fayre on days	Or have me fair during the days
And on nyghtes on the fowlyst wyfe -	And on nights be the foulest wife -
The one ye must nedes have.	One of there you needs must have.
Chese the one or the oder.	Choose one or the other.
Chese on, Sir Knyght, whiche you is levere...'	Choose on, sir knight, whichever you prefer...'

(629-666 Thomas Hahn, Author's modernization)

When Gawain leaves the choice to his wife, she claims that he has given her "sovereynté serteyn" (701), and this releases the curse upon her.

The Marriage of Sir Gawaine (Anonymous)

Summary

King Arthur is celebrating Christmas at Carlisle when a beautiful young woman enters the court and asks for a boon. Her love has been taken away by a giant knight whose castle is at Tearne-Wadling. This knight has defied King Arthur to avenge the young woman. Arthur immediately calls for Excalibur and his armor and he rides out to confront the knight. However, when Arthur does so he finds his strength magically drained away. At the knight's mercy, Arthur agrees to answer the question: 'What thing it is all women most desire?' He swears to return to Tearne-Wadling with the answer in one year. (It is only fair to add that in the original, much faded and hard to decipher manuscript, half a page, approximately nine stanzas, is missing after line ten. The version offered above is Bishop Percy's reconstruction. Arthur Quiller-Couch in *The Oxford Book of Ballads* (1910) offered another conjectural scenario that "Soon after Christmas the King chanced to ride by Tarn Wadling, in the forest of Inglewood, when he was met by a fierce baron armed with a club, who offered him choice between fighting and ransom. For ransom, the King must return on New Year's Day [with the answer to the question.]" This is now the more accepted reconstruction.)

Arthur rides east and west collecting and writing down the answers to his question, though he has no confidence in them. Finally, while he is crossing a moor, between an oak and a holly tree, Arthur sees a hideous woman who promises to ease his pain. Arthur vows that if she can help him he will grant her any wish. The old woman tells him the secret of women's desires and then asks for the hand of a young, fair, and courtly knight in marriage. Arthur returns to Tearne-Wadling where he recites all of the answers he has learned, but only last does he give the loathly lady's answer which proves to be correct. The knight angrily tells Arthur that the old hag is his sister and vows vengeance on her.

Arthur returns to Carlisle and recounts his adventures. When he hears of Arthur's promise to the loathly lady, the gentile knight Sir Gawain volunteers to marry her despite Arthur's graphic description of her ugliness. The following day, Arthur, Gawain and other knights go to find the old hag. When they see her, the other knights vow that they would never marry her, but despite her hideous appearance Gawain remains true to his word.

Gawain marries the loathly lady, and on their wedding night, she becomes the most beautiful woman he has ever seen. Gawain is amazed and delighted; he kisses her again and again. The young woman tells him to choose whether he would have her beautiful by day and ugly by night, or vice versa. Gawain considers the two alternatives, but to him they each appear impossible, so he gives his wife *her* will by asking her to choose.

The wife tells Gawain that by his answer he willl have her always beautiful. She explains that her hateful stepmother cast a spell of ugliness on her, which would only be broken when a gentle knight married her and allowed himself to be ruled in their marriage by her. At the same time, her brother was placed under a spell which forced him to live by rapine and wrong. Gawain's action has also freed him from this spell.

The Marriage of Gawain and *The Wife of Bath's Tale* Compared

As with the other two tales, there is no meaningful context for the theme of sovereignty/mastery in *The Marriage of Gawain* because the spell under which the loathly lady lives is an arbitrary act by her stepmother. There is no narrative or thematic connection between the question posed to Arthur by the loathly lady's brother and the question which she poses to Gawain on their marriage bed.

Unlike the other two tales, the quest is begun by a wronged maiden seeking redress at the court of Arthur, which recalls the maiden in Alison's tale. Both young women simply disappear from the action having set events in motion, but the young maiden in *The Marriage of Gawain* has not been harmed by Gawain, and even more strongly than in the other two tales Gawain is simply rewarded (by getting a beautiful young wife) for his existing nobility not for his reformation. In none of these three stories do the women of Camelot have the crucial role which the Wife of Bath gives them.

As in Alison's tale, the old hag tells Arthur the answer to the question secretly and the reader only learns what she has said when Arthur tells the knight who threatens his life that the woman he met. The Middle English requires no modernization:

> '... sayes, all women will have their wille,
> This is their chief desyre;'
> (Percy)

In answer to his wife's beauty day or night question, Gawain repeats the same term:

> 'My faire ladyè, sir Gawaine sayd,
> I yield me to thy skille;
> Because thou art mine owne ladyè
> Thou shalt have all thy wille.'
> (Percy)

as does the wife in her explanation that she must remain under the terms of her curse until her husband

> '... wolde yielde to be rul'd by mee,
> And let mee have all my wille.'
> (Percy)

The term 'will' is perhaps simpler than either 'mastery' or 'sovereignty' and so fits more easily into a ballad. The meaning is, however, the same.

As with the other two tales, the ugliness of the Loathly Lady is described at length. This is the description when Arthur first meets her:

Her nose was crookt and turnd outwàrde,
Her chin stoode all awrye;
And where as sholde have been her mouthe,
Lo! there was set her eye:

Her haires, like serpents, clung aboute
Her cheekes of deadlye hewe:
A worse-form'd ladye than she was,
No man mote ever viewe.
(Percy)

An innovation in *The Marriage of Gawain* is to have Gawain accompanied by a number of knights whose horror at the sight of the old hag gives further emphasis to the nobility of Gawain in sticking to his promise to marry her:

Sir Kay beheld that lady's face,
And looked upon her sweere;
Whoever kisses that ladye, he sayes,
Of his kisse he stands in feare.

Sir Kay beheld that ladye againe,
And looked upon her snout;
Whoever kisses that ladye, he sayes,
Of his kisse he stands in doubt.

Peace, brother Kay, sayde sir Gawàine,
And amend thee of thy life:
For there is a knight amongst us all,
Must marry her to his wife.

What marry this foule queane, quoth Kay,
I' the devil's name anone;
Gett mee a wife wherever I maye,
In sooth shee shall be none.

Then some tooke up their hawkes in haste,
And some took up their houndes;
And sayd they wolde not marry her,
For cities, nor for townes.
(Percy)

Though the marriage of the two and the consequences of Gawain giving his wife her will are dealt with in a most profunctory manner, the sequence of transition from hag to beautiful maiden and question is exactly as in the other two tales. The reader is, however, given a little more insight into the dilemma which his wife's question causes Gawain as he evaluates each of the two alternatives:

> Sir Gawaine scant could lift his head,
> For sorrowe and for care;
> When, lo! instead of that lothelye dame,
> Hee sawe a young ladye faire.

> Sweet blushes stayn'd her rud-red cheeke,
> Her eyen were blacke as sloe:
> The ripening cherrye swellde her lippe,
> And all her necke was snowe.

> Sir Gawaine kiss'd that lady faire,
> Lying upon the sheete:
> And swore, as he was a true knighte,
> The spice was never soe sweete.

> Sir Gawaine kiss'd that lady brighte,
> Lying there by his side:
> 'The fairest flower is not soe faire:
> Thou never can'st bee my bride.'

> 'I am thy bride, mine owne deare lorde,
> The same whiche thou didst knowe,
> That was soe lothlye, and was wont
> Upon the wild more to goe.

> 'Nowe, gentle Gawaine, chuse,' quoth shee,
> 'And make thy choice with care;
> Whether by night, or else by daye,
> Shall I be foule or faire?'

> 'To have thee foule still in the night,
> When I with thee should playe!
> I had rather farre, my lady deare,
> To have thee foule by daye.'

> 'What when gaye ladyes goe with their lords
> To drinke the ale and wine;
> Alas! then I must hide myself,
> I must not goe with mine?

> 'My faire ladyè, sir Gawaine sayd,
> I yield me to thy skille;
> Because thou art mine owne ladyè
> Thou shalt have all thy wille."

Nowe blessed be thou, sweete Gawàine,
And the daye that I thee see;
For as thou seest mee at this time,
Soe shall I ever bee.
(Percy)

Conclusion

In all three tales, as soon as the man gives up mastery, his wife becomes dutiful and obedient, but only in the Chaucer version does this really make sense.

Appendix One: The Friar in *The General Prologue*

[Friars] preach poverty to us, but they always have their hand stretched out to receive riches ... Oh, how the friar conducts himself when he comes to a poor house! Oh, how he knows how to give a sermon! Even if the lady has little or nothing ... [he] takes a halfpenny if she does not have penny... (John Gower *The Mirror of Mankind* Norton Anthology)

I found there friars from each of the four orders,
Preaching to the people for their personal profit,
Interpreting the Gospel just as they saw fit,
Desiring apparel for themselves, they twisted it as they liked.
Many of these master friars wear what they choose,
For to them money and preaching go together.
(Langland. *The Vision of Piers Plowman* Author's modernization)

It is not just a clash of personalities which accounts for the conflict between the Wife of Bath and the Friar. Both as a cleric and as a serial seducer of women, the Friar represents everything in a male-dominated society against which Alison rebels.

In Chaucer's England, there were four orders of Friars: Franciscans, Dominicans, Carmelites, and Augustinians. Monks and friars took similar vows of poverty, chastity and obedience to the rules of their order, but, unlike monks, friars went out into the world to minister to the spiritual needs of the laity, particularly the poor and the sick. This meant that they duplicated the role of parsons in preaching, saying mass, taking confession, and accepting offerings, and this was the cause of some resentment.

The Mendicant Friars (Franciscans and Dominicans) lived by begging, but this activity, which St. Francis had allowed only when actually necessary, had by Chaucer's time become very profitable, so much so that friars purchased the exclusive begging rights to an area from their order. The potential for corruption was enormous since there was no way to check on the amount which the friar actually raised by begging over and above what he paid for his license (Bowden *Guide* 57).

Probably the most famous friar in medieval literature is Friar Tuck who appears in the tales of Robin Hood and is noted for his humor and his love of good food and wine. However, as Pollard notes, "about the time Chaucer wrote, they [friars] must have been especially unpopular, as in 1385, in consequence of riots in which their houses were pulled down, a proclamation had to be issued for their protection" (52).

Chaucer's description of the Friar from *The General Prologue*:

There was a Friar, easygoing and merry,
Who was a limiter [i.e., licensed to beg within a particular, or limited, district], a very impressive man.
210   In all of the four orders of Friars there was none who knew
So much about sweet conversation and fine language.
He had arranged a number of marriages
For young women and paid all the expenses out of his own pocket.
He was the pillar of his Order.
215   He had a close friendship
With the franklins in his district
And also with the women of high social standing in the town;
He had the power of taking Confession for serious sins
As he said himself, with more authority than the parish priest,
220   Because he was licensed by his Order.
He heard Confession in a very gentle way
And getting absolution from him was a pleasure;
He was an easy man when it came to giving out punishments
Wherever he knew he would get plenty of money.
225   To give a donation to a poor Order
Is a sure sign that a man is truly repentant
For if a man offered a gift after confession
The Friar was ready to vouch that he really was sorry for what he'd done;
Because many men's hearts are so hard
230   That they cannot cry, although their sin hurts them deeply.
Therefore instead of crying and praying
Men must give silver to the poor Friars.
His cape was stuffed full of knives
And pins to give to fair young women.
235   Certainly he had a very pleasant voice;
He sang and played well
And at singing popular songs he was the best.

His neck was as white as the lily;
He was as strong as a professional fighter.
240 He knew well all of the taverns in every town
And every innkeeper and barmaid
Better than any lepers of beggar women;
For such an important man as he
It was not appropriate, he thought,
245 To be acquainted with sick lepers.
It was not respectable or profitable
To have dealings with such poor people,
But only with rich people and food merchants.
And wherever profit was likely
250 He was courteous and humble in his manners.
Nowhere was there any man so effective.
He was the best beggar in his friary;
And paid a rent for begging rights;
No other friars dared to come onto his patch;
255 Even if a widow was extremely poor
So pleasant his reading of 'In principio'
He would have a farthing before he left her.
What he made from begging was much more than he paid for his
begging license.
He knew how to play just like a puppy.
260 He was very useful at love days [days appointed for the settlement of
disputes by arbitration]
For he was not like a person locked away in a cloister
With a threadbare old cloak like a poor scholar,
But he dressed like a Master of Arts or a Pope.
His cloak was made of fine heavy wool
265 It was rounded like a bell just out of the mould.
He lisped a little, out of affectation,
To make his English sound sweet on his tongue;
And when playing the harp after he had sung
His eyes twinkled in his head just
270 Like the stars in the frosty night.
This worthy limiter was called Hubert.
(Author's modernization)

The Friar's sexuality is spelled out in the clearest terms. Firstly, he is shown to be expert at seducing women with his love-making and false promises:

In alle the ordres foure is noon that kan
So muchel of daliaunce and fair langage. (210-11)

It seems ironically superfluous to comment that he is the most skillful seducer in the four orders of friars, since (at least in theory) there should be relatively little competition. The Friar is shown to travel prepared with seduction gifts, kept ironically in the hood of his habit:

His tipet was ay farsed ful of knives
And pinnes, for to yeven faire wives. (233-4)

It is a subtle touch by the Poet to make the point that the Friar can afford to be choosy: he is interested only in attractive women. Nor does the Poet avoid the consequences of the Friar's sexual promiscuity, although he deals with it euphemistically: young girls get pregnant, and he buys them off by securing them a husband and paying the expenses of the marriage. The register of the Bishop of Bath and Wells for 1321 records the case of a friar who had reneged on his promise to provide a dowry for a young woman by whom he had fathered two children (Bowden *Commentary* 124):

He hadde maad ful many a marriage
Of yonge wommen at his owene cost.
Unto his ordre he was a noble post. (212-4)

The praise-line which follows the details of the Friar's sexual corruption gains obvious irony by the juxtaposition. The reader must decide whether the metaphor of the Friar as a pillar or column is a phallic joke – for myself, I have not the faintest doubt of it.

The Poet's final comment on the Friar's sexuality is the height of ironic understatement:

In love-dayes ther koude he muchel help, (260)

Jane Austen, no less, defined love-days as "a day formerly appointed for an amicable adjustment of differences." Bowden points out that a love-day was a day appointed by the civil courts for the amicable reconciliation of specific court cases, and thus that the Friar meddles in civil affairs, "an act expressly forbidden in the Rules of the Mendicant Orders" (*Guide* 59). The practice of love-days had fallen into disrepute long before Chaucer's day having declined into bribery, coercion, and the victory of the more powerful party in the dispute. The Poet's irony rests on the fact that, while it would indeed be appropriate for a friar to use his position and his negotiating skills to bring together arguing factions, this Friar, who actually abuses his skills and position of trust to seduce young women, would certainly enter fully into the profitable corruption of love-days.

The description of the Friar's clothing is satirical:

> His tipet was ay farsed ful of knives
> And pinnes, for to yeven faire wives.
> … he was nat lik a cloisterer
> With a thredbare cope, as is a povre scoler,
> But he was lyk a maister or a pope.
> Of double worstede was his semicope,
> That rounded as a belle out of the presse.
> (233-4 and 261-5)

The exact nature of a "tipet" is a little unclear, but the Ellesmere Manuscript shows the Friar wearing a very loose hood which drapes like a stole on his shoulders. At the rear, the hood falls half-way down the Friar's back forming a very deep 'pocket' in which he carries his seduction gifts forming a visual symbol of the way in which this man perverts the rule of his order for his own pleasure and self-interest. His habit appears in the illustration to have decorative trimming: it is said to be made of the finest quality woolen cloth and to be trimmed with fur. He does not simply break the rules of his Order; he flouts them.

Appendix Two: Guide to Further Reading

The Chaucer literature is vast, but much of it is written by specialists for specialists. An additional problem for the reader/student seeking an introduction to *The Wife of Bath's Prologue and Tale* is the fact that, since most books deal with the whole of *The Canterbury Tales* (if not the whole of Chaucer's literary output), they tend to contain only a section on the *Prologue and Tale*.

The works selected appear to me to offer a great place to start.

Works on *The Canterbury Tales* as a whole:

Laura and Robert Lambdin's *Chaucer's Pilgrims A Historical Guide to the Pilgrims in The Canterbury Tales* (1999) - brings Manly's approach up to date.

Muriel Bowden's *A Commentary on the General Prologue* - still the best single volume on the *Prologue* - emphasizes the historical background to the pilgrims – exhaustively documented.

Peter Brown's *A Companion to Chaucer* (2002) - a huge book but, it has a great index and can be read selectively.

Ray Moore's *"The General Prologue" by Geoffrey Chaucer: A Critical Introduction* (2013) - a clearly written and comprehensive critical introduction.

Works on *The Wife of Bath's Prologue and Tale*:

Kolve and Olson's Norton Critical Edition *Geoffrey Chaucer The Canterbury Tales Fifteen Tales and The General Prologue* provides a clear texts and modernized versions of all significant sources and background texts.

Bibliography

Works on *The Canterbury Tales* as a whole:

Baldwin, Ralph. *The Unity of The Canterbury Tales*. 1st ed. Copenhagen: Rosenkilde and Bagger, 1955. Print.

Benson, C. David. *Chaucer's Drama of Style Poetic Variety and Contrast in the Canterbury Tales*. 1st ed. Chapel Hill: University of North Carolina Press, 1986. Print.

Bloom, Harold, ed. *Geoffrey Chaucer*. 1st ed. Broomall: Chelsea House Publishers, 1999. Print.

Bloom, Harold, ed. *Bloom's Modern Critical Interpretations Geoffrey Chaucer The Canterbury Tales*. New Edition. New York: Infobase Publishing, 2008. Print.

Bloom, Harold, ed. *Modern Critical Interpretations Geoffrey Chaucer's The General Prologue to the Canterbury Tales*. 1st ed. New York: Chelsea House Publishers, 1988. Print.

Boitani, Piero, and Jill Mann, eds. *The Cambridge Companion to Chaucer*. 5th printing. Cambridge: Cambridge University Press, 2008. Print.

Muriel Bowden's *A Commentary on the General Prologue to the Canterbury Tales*. 2nd ed. London: MacMillan Company. 1969. Print.

Bowden, Muriel. *A Reader's Guide to Geoffrey Chaucer*. 1st ed. New York: Farrar, Straus and Giroux, 1964. Print.

Brewer, Derek. *Chaucer and His World*. 1st ed. New York: Dodd, Mead & Company, 1978. Print.

Brown, Peter, and Andrew Butcher. *The Age of Saturn Literature and History in The Canterbury Tales*. 1st ed. Cambridge: Basil Blackwell, 1991. Print.

Brown, Peter ed.. *A Companion to Chaucer*. 1st ed. Malden: Blackwell Publishing, 2002. Print.

Clements, John. "The Sword & Buckler Tradition - Part 1." *ARMA*. The Association for Renaissance Martial Arts, 1999. Web. 17 Jun 2012.

Cooper, Helen. *Oxford Guides to Chaucer The Canterbury Tales*. 2nd ed. New York: Oxford University Press, 1996. Print.

Davis, Norman, Douglas Gray, Patricia Ingham and Alice Hadril. *A Chaucer Glossary*. 1st ed. Oxford: Clarendon Press, 1979/ Print.

Del Dotto, Darcy, and Hailey Prescott. "Rouncy." *Horses in Medieval Times*. Massachusetts Academy of Math and Science, n.d. Web. 22 May 2012.

Forkin, Thomas. "Essays in Medieval Studies." *Essays in Medieval Studies* . Volume 24. (2007): 31-41. Print.

Gies , Frances, and Joseph Gies. *Daily Life in Medieval Times*. 1st ed. New York: Barnes & Noble Books, 1990. Print.

Gilbert, Rosalie. "Sumptuary Laws." *ROSALIE'S MEDIEVAL WOMAN*. Rosalie Gilbert, n.d. Web. 26 Nov 2012.

Hallissy, Margaret, *A Companion to Chaucer's Canterbury Tales*. 1st ed. Westport: Greenwood, 1995. Print.

Halveron, John. *Geoffrey Chaucer The Canterbury Tales*. 1st ed. Indianapolis: Bobbs-Merrill Company, 1971. Print.

Hirsh, John. *Chaucer and the Canterbury Tales A Short Introduction*. 1st ed. Malden: Blackwell Publishing, 2003. Print.

Hodges, Laura. *Chaucer And Clothing: Clerical And Academic Costume In The General Prologue To The Canterbury Tales*. 1st ed. Cambridge: D. S. Brewer, 2005. Print.

Howard, Donald. "The Idea of *The Canterbury Tales*." *Modern Critical Views: Geoffrey Chaucer*. Ed. Harold Bloom. 1st ed. New York: Chelsea House Publishers, 1985. 79-104. Print.

Kittredge, George. *Chaucer and His Poetry*. 55th Anniversary Edition. Cambridge: Harvard University Press, 1970. Print.

Lambdin, Laura, and Robert Lambdin, eds. *Chaucer's Pilgrims A Historical Guide to the Pilgrims in The Canterbury Tales*. 1st ed. Westport: Praeger, 1999. Print.

Manly, John. *Some New Light on Chaucer*. Reprint of 1st ed. Gloucester: Peter Smith, 1959. Print.

"Medieval Estates and Orders - Making and Breaking Rules: Texts and Contexts." *The Norton Anthology of English Literature*. W.W. Norton and Company. Web. 27 Nov 2012.

Miller, Robert. *Chaucer Sources and Backgrounds*. 1st ed. New York: Oxford University Press, 1977. Print.

Moore, Raymond, *The General Prologue by Geoffrey Chaucer: A Critical Introduction* 1st ed. Self-published, 2013. Print.

170

Patterson, Lee. *Geoffrey Chaucer's The Canterbury Tales: A Casebook*. 1st ed. New York: Oxford University Press, 2007. Print.

Pollard, Alfred. *Chaucer's Canterbury Tales: The Prologue*, 1st ed. London: Macmillan, 1903. Print.

Rossignol, Rosalyn. *Critical Companion to Chaucer: A Literary Reference to His Life and Work.*1st ed. New York, Infobase, 2007. Print.

Rudd, Gillian. *The Complete Critical Guide to Geoffrey Chaucer*. 1st ed. London: Routledge, 2001. Print.

Shuster, Allison, Kristen Zaki, and Arianne Traurig. "Chaucer's Pilgrims and Their Clothing." *Medieval Literature and Material Culture* . N.p.. Web. 13 Nov 2012.

Wetherbee, Winthrop. *Geoffrey Chaucer The Canterbury Tales*. 2nd ed. Cambridge: Cambridge University Press, 2004. Print.

Wilcockson, Colin. *Geoffrey Chaucer The Canterbury Tales A Selection*. 1st ed., London: Penguin Books, 2008. Print.

Williams, David. *The Canterbury Tales: A Literary Pilgrimage*. 1st ed. Boston: Twayne Publishers, 1987. Print.

Other Middle English Texts

In Chapter 7:

The extracts from John Gower's "Tale of Florent" are in John Gower's *Confessio amantis* published by The Oxford Clarendon Press, 1899-1902 reproduced at "Corpus of Middle English Prose and Verse", UR http://quod.lib.umich.edu/c/cme/

The extracts from "The Wedding of Gawain and Dame Ragnelle," are in *Sir Gawain: Eleven Romances and Tales*, ed. Thomas Hahn (Kalamazoo, MI: Medieval Institute Publications, 1995). Copyright 1995 by the Board of the Medieval Institute.

The extracts from "The Marriage of Gawain" are in *Reliques of Ancient English Poetry* collected and edited by Bishop Thomas Percy published 1765. So far as I am aware, this work is not subject to copyright.

Works on *The Wife of Bath's Prologue and Tale*

Editions of the Text

Cigman, Gloria. Ed. *The Wife of Bath's Prologue and Tale and The Clerk's Prologue and Tale from The Canterbury Tales*. 1st ed. New York: Holmes and Meier, 1975. Print.

Kolve, V. A. and Glending Olson. Ed. *Geoffrey Chaucer The Canterbury Tales Fifteen Tales and The General Prologue*. 2nd ed. New York: W. W. Norton, 2005. Print.

Critical Works

William, Robert. Chainani, Soman ed. "The Canterbury Tales Study Guide : Summary and Analysis of The Wife of Bath's Tale". GradeSaver, 30 November 2008 Web. 10 December 2013.

About the Author

Ray Moore was born in Nottingham, England in 1950. He obtained his Master's Degree in Literature at Lancaster University in 1974 and then taught in secondary education for twenty-eight years before relocating to Florida with his wife in 2002. There he taught English and Information Technology in the International Baccalaureate Program at Vanguard High School in Ocala.

He retired in June 2012 and is now a full-time writer and fitness fanatic.

Website: http://www.raymooreauthor.com

If you have any comments about this book *please* contact the author through his email: moore.ray1@yahoo.com

Also written by Ray Moore:

All books are available from amazon.com and from barnesandnoble.com as paperbacks and at most online ebook retailers.

Fiction:

The Lyle Thorne Mysteries: each book features five tales from the Golden Age of Detection:

Investigations of The Reverend Lyle

Further Investigations of The Reverend Lyle Thorne

Early Investigations of Lyle Thorne

Sanditon Investigations of The Reverend Lyle Thorne (to be published late summer 2014)

Non-fiction:

The Critical Introduction series is written for high school teachers and students and for college undergraduates. Each volume gives an in-depth analysis of a key text:

"The Stranger" by Albert Camus: A Critical Introduction

"The General Prologue" by Geoffrey Chaucer: A Critical Introduction

"Pride and Prejudice" by Jane Austen: A Critical Introduction

"The Great Gatsby" by F. Scott Fitzgerald: A Critical Introduction

"The Wife of Bath's Prologue and Tale" by Geoffrey Chaucer: Text and Critical Introduction

"Sir Gawain and the Green Knight": Text and Critical Introduction

"The General Prologue" by Geoffrey Chaucer: Text and Critical Introduction

Other Study Guides available as e-books:

"The Myth of Sisyphus" and "The Stranger" by Albert Camus: Two Study Guides
"Of Mice and Men" by John Steinbeck: A Study Guide
"The Pearl" by John Steinbeck: A Study Guide
"Great Expectations" by Charles Dickens: A Study Guide
"Jane Eyre" by Charlotte Brontë: A Study Guide
"Wuthering Heights" by Emily Brontë: A Study Guide
"The Mill on the Floss" by George Eliot: A Study Guide
"Catch-22" by Joseph Heller: A Study Guide
"Slaughterhouse-Five" by Kurt Vonnegut: A Study Guide

Teacher resources:

Ray also publishes many more study guides and other resources for classroom use on the 'Teacher Pay Teachers' website:

http://www.teacherspayteachers.com/Store/Raymond-Moore

Printed in Great Britain
by Amazon.co.uk, Ltd.,
Marston Gate.